D1807634

WORDS FROM MY BELLY

WORDS FROM MY BELLY

Telly Timpson

Copyright © 2019 by Telly Timpson.

Library of Congress Control Number:		2019904052
ISBN:	Hardcover	978-1-7960-2563-7
	Softcover	978-1-7960-2564-4
	eBook	978-1-7960-2565-1

All rights reserved. No part of this book may be reproduced or transmitted
in any form or by any means, electronic or mechanical, including photocopying,
recording, or by any information storage and retrieval system,
without permission in writing from the copyright owner.

Christian Standard Bible (CSB)
The Christian Standard Bible. Copyright © 2017 by Holman Bible Publishers.
Used by permission. Christian Standard Bible®, and CSB® are federally
registered trademarks of Holman Bible Publishers, all rights reserved.

Any people depicted in stock imagery provided by Getty Images are models,
and such images are being used for illustrative purposes only.
Certain stock imagery © Getty Images.

Print information available on the last page.

Rev. date: 04/07/2019

To order additional copies of this book, contact:
Xlibris
1-888-795-4274
www.Xlibris.com
Orders@Xlibris.com
793843

CONTENTS

CHAPTER 1: DEVOTION

CHAPTER 2: THOUGHTS

CHAPTER 3: WISDOM

CHAPTER 4: STORM

CHAPTER 5: WARFARE

CHAPTER 6: FOR HER

CHAPTER 7: 4 YOUR SOUL

INTRODUCTION

This book is a collection of poems that I had written over the years. Each poem is a window to what I was going through or experienced at that time. This book was designed to encourage you through your hard times and also usher you into worship. The main reason for this book manifesting in such a time is to give glory to God. God has brought me out of so many emotional roller coasters—people hating me and speaking all matters of evil against me, bad relationships, fighting myself, fighting the enemy, and fighting who I am in God. I pray to God and my Lord and Savior Jesus Christ that this book will have you in your walk toward your destiny but most of all your relationship with God the Father, God the Son, and God the Holy Spirit. Stay blessed!

CHAPTER 1

Devotion

CLAY ON MY EYES

Lord, put clay on my eyes,
I have been blinded by this world,
Lord, put clay on my eyes,
So my spiritual eye can unfurl,
Most of my life I've been walking by sight & not by faith,
Getting trapped in snares & making mistake after mistake,
Lord, put clay on my eyes,
So I can regain my spiritual sight,
Let me go to the fountain,
So I can wash my eyes to see the Light,
So I can behold Your presence,
To stand in awe and reverence,
Too long I had been making decisions,
Based upon my worldly vision,
Now I want to make a circumcision,
Of that view and embrace You,
Lord, remove this fleshly blindfold,
So that my third eye can behold,
The spiritual realm with You God is at the helm,
I thank you God for being on Your side,
Lord please put that holy clay on my eyes.

Words from My Belly Devotional

Clay on My Eyes

Scripture: John 9:6–7 (CSB): "After He said these things He spit on the ground, made some mud from the saliva, and spread the mud on his eyes. 7) 'Go,' He told him, '**wash in the pool Siloam**' [which means 'Sent']. So he left, washed, and came back seeing."

Testimony

I wrote this poem in a time in my life where I really desired to see things in the Spirit. The inspiration of the came from John 9:6–7, when Jesus spit on the ground to make mud, placed the mud on the blind man's eyes, told him to wash his eyes, and now he is able to see. In my case, the blindness was my worldview or the view that world had given me. It was like a blindfold to the things or moves of God in my life or those who are close to me. Have you ever had a one-track mind or one view and knew nothing else but that mind-set? Romans 12:2 states, *"**Do not be conformed to this world, but be transformed by the renewing of your mind, so that you may discern what is the good, pleasing, and perfect will of GOD.**"* The renewal of the mind is my renewing my view. When God opened my eyes to my understanding, I started seeing things in a different light. I was able to see!

I Need Thee!

As I sit alone, my mind rewinds. As I mentally observe my history, Lord, I seek Your face more than Your hand. I am weak, Lord, help me stand. Too many times I seek things that are tangible, when I know You are incredible. Lord, I am laying and crying for Your help to die to self, words spoken to my ear to fear but Your voice in sincere. As my physical form is in a position of humility, Your voice is saying to be still in me. I understand what You are saying, but my flesh is playing. It wants to do the opposite of what You say, but it is broken, so my flesh lay. Laying prostrate on the ground where it came from, I command it to be silent, mute, and dumb. To You, oh my Lord, Your face I seek, but first I minister to You by kissing Your feet. Father, my tears of joy rain down on Your foot, the hairs of my gratitude wipe Your toes. The oil anointing wants to fragrance Your feet even at the soles. I need You, Lord, today, tomorrow is not promised, and yesterday has gone away. I am knocking at Your throne room door needing You more; please restore. Restore my passion and my likeness of You; I'd painted myself an identity looking like a clown or a fool. I need Thee: I love You so much; I come before You desiring Your divine touch. Break these bounds, I need to be free! I can't say it enough, I need Thee!

Words from My Belly Devotional

<u>I Need Thee!</u>

Scripture: Psalm 72:12: "For he will rescue the poor who cry out and the afflicted who have no helper."

Testimony

I wrote this poem in a time of desperation. I really, really—I mean really—needed the Lord. I couldn't control myself, asking why I was acting in a negative matter. My flesh was taking control, mind you. I was saved and Holy Ghost–filled. I allowed my flesh to take control over me; "me" was not my body but my spirit. I didn't read the Word like I was supposed to, didn't worship like I used to, and was slowly drifting back to my old habits. I made a choice to forget about everything and seek God. It was not pretty; all I know was I needed Him! If you feel like you're slowly drifting away from God, abandon everything and seek God. The Bible says in Luke 11:9, "*So I say to you, keeping asking, and it will be given to you. Keep searching and you find. Keep knocking, and the door will be opened.*" I know for myself, I am a man, but when it comes to seeking God, macho is out the door. I need Him!

Revealed in the Secret Place

What a wonderful thing to be able to dwell in the secret place of the Most High God,
To be covered by His mighty wing,
This place, where there is peace but not just any peace,
A peace that surpasses all understanding,
As you minister to the Father, He is ministering back to you at the same time,
My soul gets upset when I have to leave this place,
I am addicted to Him as a junkie to drugs,
I can't live without Him; I can't imagine life without Him,
Beyond this mortal coil, the secret place where things are revealed,
Where your flesh ends and your healing begins,
What a place!
I've been walking away from the door of access where my answers and peace dwells,
I am running, run, run, run, running to the door to enter in,
Silence . . . silence . . . silence,
Quietness is kept,
Shh, can you hear the sound of silence,
A wind is blowing this way, a breeze,
Take a deep inhale then exhale,
Peace of mind, body, and spirit,
Hear the new sound in the earth,
A spiritual sound,
Listen . . . listen, it draws near, it is just over the horizon,
Shh, listen . . . your belly wants to speak with a new sound,

Listen, it is right there . . . right there,
Belly talk . . .
In the place, this secret place of the Most High,
The place where the hungry and thirsty abide,
Secrets are revealed for this race,
The secret place, my place, His place.

Words from My Belly Devotional

Revealed in the Secret Place

Scripture: Daniel 2:22: "He reveals the deep and hidden things; He knows what is in darkness, and light dwells with HIM."

Testimony

In this poem, I was reflecting on the time I was in worship. Being in the presence of God was an awesome experience, just to be propelled into His glory. As I was reflecting, I was worshiping and I didn't realize it. I was reminded of a scripture in Isaiah 26:3: **"You will keep in perfect peace the mind [that is] dependant [on You], for it is trusting in You."** When I am in God's, presence, He reveals His peace that surpasses all understanding. I find it hard to leave God's presence and go back to this reality. But I love going there.

By Your Waters

I am walking through the wilderness of my life guided by my Comforter,
He led me to a river of gold,
This river is untouched by the fleshly hands of man,
The sound of the water flowing downstream calms my soul,
Then, a still, small voice spoke to me and said, "Taste and see,"
So I got down on my knees asking Him,
"Am I worthy to receive?"
He said, "Drink and never thirst,"
"The Blood of my Son freed you from sin's curse,"
"I had called you by My name,"
"I am He who ordains,"
So I took a drink from the river of gold,
Oh, how it fills my soul!
It was by Your waters I found peace,
It was by Your waters I received increase,
Increase of Your love,
The wind of Your breath whirls around me
and embraces me like a fatherly hug,
You lead me to a place of Your glory,
Forever restoring me; I have to tell the story,
The secret place You have taken me,
I don't want to depart from this sanctuary,
The sanctuary of Your loving arms,
Where I found safety from harm,
If this is a dream, let me not wake up,
I am so addicted to Your touch,
Touch me, Lord, the only way You can!

By Your mighty yet gentle hand,
You have been my Father, Master, Comforter, and Friend,
Please, oh Lord! Don't let this romance come to a premature end,
Thank You, Lord, for taking me to this liquid border,
This place of Yours, by Your Waters.

Words from My Belly Devotional

By Your Waters

Scripture: Psalm 23:1–3: "The LORD is my shepherd; there is nothing I lack. 2) He lets me lie down in green pastures; He leads me beside quiet waters. He renews my life; He leads me along the right paths for HIS name's sake."

Testimony

I know God as a restorer of strength. In times of worship, I experience a refresh not just in my spirit but my body. The water could mean many things to a lot of people. The water in this poem means God's love, Jesus's blood, and the Holy Spirit's restoring flood. I didn't mean to rhyme like that, but hey, I am a poet. If you were outside in the middle of summer for an hour, the sun is blazing, and you run to your house to your refrigerator where there is cold bottled water. You take that water, rip the cap open, and drink it. Didn't that water refresh you? It is like the Spirit; when everyday living gets hot, you can run to that refrigerator called prayer and drink that refreshing water and call on God's presence to restore you.

L-O-V-E

If I can express this emotion in terms somewhat educational,
But I am not because God's love is unconditional,
Correlating my thoughts and feelings in this script of words,
Expressing inner affections unheard,
I am failing in my mission in verbalizing,
It is difficult, now I am realizing,
How can you describe the indescribable?
How can you find the right adjective to label the incredible?
Love, an emotion most misunderstood by meaning,
God is love; it is in the Bible reading,
I don't try in my quest to describe,
All I know is, in His arms I want to abide,
I am a Longing, Obedient, Vessel Exposed,
I don't care who knows,
He is a God that I am not ashamed of,
He wasn't ashamed of me when He sent an example of His love,
His only Son that was begotten,
To go into a world to die because it was rotten,
Lord, I am Longing for Your touch,
Being Obedient to Your Word which I've learned so much,
I am a Vessel waiting to be used,
Exposed for You, I don't care, take me through,
Administrate my life, Lord, according to Your will,
With Your love and anointing in this broken vessel please fill,
If it pleases You, I will let the World know,
Because of Your love,
I am a Longing, Obedient, Vessel Exposed.

Words from My Belly Devotional

L-O-V-E

Scripture: Ephesians 2:10: "For we are His Creation-created in Christ JESUS for the good works, which GOD prepared ahead of time so that we should walk in them."

Testimony

This poem expresses how much I love God and how I desire to be used by Him. Longing, Obedient, Vessel, Exposed. Longing is my inward desire for God. Obedient is what I have to be in order to be used by Him. Vessel is what I am waiting to be filled by what is eternal. Exposed is me being sent into a world that rejects the teaching of the Bible along with my mess; I want to let the world know I go through the same thing they do, but I have Jesus who gives me peace through it all.

The Weight of Your Glory

Lord, the weight of your glory is too much to bear,
All I can do is humble myself and stare,
At Your majestic light so bright,
That chases away the night,
What a wondrous sight,
The weight of Your glory is beyond measure,
Beyond the pleasures of this earth,
I am not worthy to be in Your presence,
Next to royalty, I am but a peasant,
The weight of Your glory is heavy but not a burden,
Your yoke is easy, I know that for certain,
I am standing in awe of Your glory like a moth to a flame,
To dance around, never wanting to leave or refrain,
The weight of Your glory is overwhelming,
Knees are bent and souls are falling down to lay prostrate at Your feet,
Near Your glory where there is relief,
In the mist of Your glory it is hard to stand,
It doesn't matter if it's a boy, girl, woman, or man,
The weight of Your glory I can't help but bow down,
Face first to the ground,
Giving you verbs, adjectives, and nouns,
My lips will continually tell the story,
Of this weight of Your glory.

Words from My Belly Devotional

The Weight of Your Glory

Scripture: Psalm 138:5: "They will sing of the LORD's ways, for the LORD's glory is great."

Testimony

In this poem, I can say this . . . I was so deep into the Lord's presence it was overwhelming. Experiencing the manifested glory of the Lord brought me to my knees and from my knees to laying prostrate. It felt like such a weight on me that I could not get up from this position. All I could do at the time was to adore Him with my words. How great is our God, very great!

Please Use Me

Lord, you made me into the person people see before them,
A cluster of living tissues, organs, and bones,
A wonder, a human being,
True, Lord, you're the Potter and I am the clay,
Day and day You change me like the weather,
Truly You are a God who is forever,
The way you put things together,
The relationship we have will never sever,
As time passes on like cars on the interstate,
I see now that I am not a mistake,
It don't matter if it is me people hate,
I am doing Your work for Your sake,
Use me as an instrument of Your glory,
And my lips will continue to tell the story,
How You save me,
How You kept me,
How You order my steps toward my destiny,
Lord, I humbly submit,
So my flesh won't exist in Your presence,
Lord, I desire to be Your tool,
To fix and to school,
Fully I don't know You,
From my birth until now I have learned a lot,
Now I can be free and out the box,
Your voice I want to hear it,
Your power has no limits,
The purpose of my life You give me a little vision,

Without you, I refuse to make a decision,
Lord, You are the Potter and I am the clay,
Grant me my daily bread this day,
I will never forget Your Son and the price He paid,
And the victory over death, hell, and the grave,
I am open, Lord, You see right through me,
I humbly ask, please use me.

Words from My Belly Devotional

<u>**Please Use Me**</u>

Scripture: Acts 9:15: "But the LORD said to him, 'Go! For this man is My chosen instrument to carry My name before the Gentiles, kings, and the sons of Israel.'"

Testimony

Have you ever wanted to be truly used by God? At this period of my life, when I wrote this poem, I was seeing others being used by God and I wanted to be used too. But I have to realize that I have to wait my turn; God has to mature in some areas of my life before I can be released to do His will and to be used by Him. The revelation didn't come until after I had written this poem. To add something else, God did not use me in the way or fashion of those who I saw being used by God.

SHEDDING

Lord, I am taking my fig leaves off. I am naked before You, exposed. I can't help but to shed this fleshy garment and make You my story, as it beckons me toward Thee. Too long I try to hide myself when I'd done wrong, when You were all the time looking for me. For a measure of time, my shame manifested a mask and with my sin cloaked. Now, my Father, I shed them and You cast them into of forgetfulness. Here I am before you naked, no more mask of shame, no more cloak of sin, and no more sandals of depression. Now You, my Father, are my obsession. No longer will I put my nametag on those filthy rags. The Blood of Jesus is my apparel that contacts the innermost parts down to the marrow. You have given me access, as I cross the threshold of Your throne room. My flesh burns off me because of Your glory; leaving my spirit only. Before You, Lord, I am exposed, uncovered, displayed, revealed, disclosed, and unmasked, willing to do Your task. Daily I die, why my flesh tries to arise when cleaning this temple for You to abide. I am standing before You, Lord, open as I can. Here I am, Lord, here I am.

Words from My Belly Devotional

Shedding

Scripture: Romans 12:1: "Therefore, brothers, by the mercies of GOD, I urge you to present your bodies as a living sacrifice, holy and pleasing to GOD; this is your spiritual worship."

Testimony

I have been a praiser for a while. My praise propelled me into His Presence, then I found out I was a worshipper. This poem was written when I transcended from flesh to spirit. You must worship God in spirit and in truth (John 4:23). I knew that my flesh, my mind, my opinion, my issue, and my will have to be cast down for me to up in Him. I dare you to just be naked (no self) before the Lord. Jesus shed His blood so that you can shed your flesh.

Talk to Me

Talk to Me,
Conversation going back and forth like ping-pong, talk to Me,
Tell Me what you feel,
I can cure what ills, talk to Me,
I'll listen to your life's mission,
That I can give you some comprehension, talk to Me,
I am here to lend an ear,
This is true and sincere, talk to Me,
Hopefully you can trust Me not to tell another living soul,
In this secret place, no farther will this conversation will go,
Talk to Me,
When you talk about it, it's your release,
To get that monkey off your back,
To rebuke that inner beast, talk to Me,
People are willing to start a conversation,
On TV or radio stations,
Airing out their dirty laundry, sex, lies, and quandaries,
Talk to Me,
Don't let the world hear your secrets,
And have them talk about you,
In Me it is well kept,
Don't be cross and upset,
I must protest and confess, talk to Me,
I have a heart that understands,
If you can, talk to Me.

Words from My Belly Devotional

Talk to Me

Scripture: 1 Peter 5:7: "[C]asting all your care upon HIM, because HE cares about you."

Testimony

Originally this poem was for this young lady I know from a few years ago. She was having some issues, and I was telling her she can "talk to me" about it. Years after I'd wrote it, I found it in my heart to change it into God telling people to talk to Him. I am encouraging you to talk to God about your problems. He always has answers; whether you like the answer or not, it is still a good answer because it comes from God.

MY DEVOTION

With my eyes lifted upward in reverence, my heart and soul press and knock at your door, longing to enter in the secret place of your Most High. I am so addicted to you, your glory, and your presence.

My knees are bent because the weight of your glory is overwhelming. I love you, Lord! I can't say it enough: I love you! As the sun rises over the hills of this world, it is telling me that your grace and mercy has kept me.

Love me, Lord! No one can touch me like You! Touch me there, right there! Where I am weak! My hands are lifted toward You, I am longing for You to take me. You romance me in the morning, You hold me at noon, and you embrace me at night. Father, you are my desire! You are the one who ignites my fire! That burns with an uncontrollable desire for You! I need Thee, oh my soul needs Thee! Your presence wraps around me! Taking me to an unknown portal of Your aroma! I am hungry for You, Father! I am starving for Your love! My spiritual throat is dry! Please quench it with the water of Your mercy! I give thanks to You!

I see Your gates with the purity of white, I push it open with my worship for You, I enter, I behold the glimpse of Your glory; I stand there in awe of You. I don't want to go! Please Lord, don't! Yes, Lord, I understand You have plans for me!

Your love is wider than the ocean,

Truly, Father, You are my devotion

Words from My Belly Devotional

My Devotion

Scripture: Matthew 22:37: "He said to him, 'Love the Lord your GOD with all your heart, with all your soul, and all your mind.'"

Testimony

What can say, I was desperate for God. Everything I ever needed, wanted, and more was God. I was very thirsty for His love, joy, glory, presence, and strength. Plain and simple, I love the Lord! Remember the time you first believed? The total and uncontrollable love you had for the Lord? For the unbeliever, I encourage you to experience God for yourself through His Son Jesus Christ; there is no way to God but through Jesus. The Bible says in Psalm 34:8, "[T]aste and see that the LORD is good."

Water Experience

Lord, Your love overwhelms me like the flood of Noah,
Drowning me with Your mercy,
As I swim deeper in the ocean of Your presence,
I find myself free,
Free to explore the depths of You,
The fortunes awaiting me that are connected to my destiny stir my curiosity,
I am floating and floating along on the current of Your will,
The whirlpool of Your glory shifts the atmosphere,
This liquid experience is enlightening,
I am in the sea of forgetfulness,
Where my sins and past troubles are laid at rest,
There at the bottom of the sea,
I see my old self decomposing,
In here, the world's cares and worries are not on my mind,
But God's love, wonders, and signs,
In this paradise of liberty,
I don't have to breathe,
God has taken my breath away,
I can stay here forever and a day,
Refreshing, restoring, a continual pouring,
This is a delight to me, to be in Your sea.

Words from My Belly **Devotional**

<u>Water Experience</u>

Scripture: Psalm 51:10: "GOD create a clean a heart for me and renew a steadfast spirit within me."

Testimony

This poem is based on a baptizing experience. Baptizing is just an outward expression of your faith. This baptizing is the Holy Spirit. There is nothing that can compare to the experience expected being in the presence of God with all His glory. It is like an inward dying; the removal of self and past issues and sins and being filled with the Holy Spirit. I was no good to no one during that. If you are not filled with the Holy Spirit, ask God to give the Spirit to you, that is, if you really want it, you got to really want it. The Bible says in Psalm 37:4, "Take delight in the LORD, and HE will give you your heart's desires."

My Adoration to You

Every day my soul is longing and wanting You. The thoughts in my head can't rest or go to bed until it's fed with Your presence. A simple whisper in my ear brings me to tears, reflecting of the years that You kept me. I am grateful that You accepted me. My passion for You knows no bounds. I need You here, I need You now! Lord, I give You the praises that are due to You. Even though my body is in pain, I still glorify You through and through. You are excepting me to fulfill my destiny, but I need Your mind to be a part of me. I long to worship You continuously, but the this vessel needs restoring. Be pleased with the fruits of my lips and the love in my heart. In the entire universe, there is nothing that can compare with Your love from the start. The love You have for me is more precious than life itself. More than this world, just thinking of You makes my heart melt. I experience Your love daily, and Your love never fails me, so I hail Thee holy. Just to be on bended knees in the Holy of Holies is all I need. I need You, Daddy! I don't care if I look foolish to man who doesn't understand Your plan. Be magnified forever, I am putting my hands together in a clap offering to You. Glory, honor, and power all belong to You. Father, You sit on the throne of my heart; there You rule. Please expect this crown of adoration to You. My Lord, Father, Master, and King, I'm glad you're mine. Lover of my soul, keeper of my mind, so beautiful and divine.

Words from My Belly Devotional

My Adoration to You

Scripture: Psalm 26:7: "[R]aising my voice in thanksgiving and telling about Your wonderful works."

Testimony

Have you given thanks to the Lord today? The Lord gives blessings after blessings each day. When you get up, that is the blessing of mercy, and when you make it through the day, that is the blessing of grace. When you are able to complete a task that seems impossible, that is the blessing of His strength. So give thanks to the One who gives good gifts to you daily.

In My Secret Closet

I enter in to enter in; I close the door behind me,
No one knows where I am; only the Lord can find me,
In this place, this secret place, this holy place,
The expectation is to behold the Father's face,
In this space that I'm in, I don't need anyone, not even a friend,
Where sin ends and worship begins,
The peace in this sacred haven is paving a foundation of love to my God
above,
Just to be under His wings propels my soul to sing,
Sing of His glory and testify how He stored me.

Oh! My soul says oh! Oh, how I adore You! I need You every day of my life.
Oh, just be wrapped in Your arms. I love you, Lord, I sing Your praises and
every day You made a way, on Your chest I want to lay. You are my passion,
my source, and my attraction. I can't help to express my deepest thoughts,
and love for You. My love, my heart's desire, my Father, my king, my Lord,
and my God. Oh God, Oh God . . .

Words from My Belly Devotional

In My Secret Closet

Scripture: Psalm 32:7: "You are hiding place; You protect me from trouble. You surround me with joyful shouts of deliverance."

Testimony

The closet is a special for me; I can go there and close the door and go for broke. At times in your life, you have to go to that secret place and shut the world off. With no distraction, you can hear God clearly. I was in that place and didn't want to leave, but I was restored to handle what life or this reality would bring. I encourage you to find that secret place; it might not be a closet, it might be your car or office. In any case, go to what you can handle what life will present to you.

You Love Me

Your love swells in me like an inflated balloon, ready to burst,
You keep blowing and blowing Your life-giving breath in me,
Refreshing me, like stepping out the shower as the coolness of the air hits my skin,
But You touch my soul, behold my flesh goes, but my spirit stays to lay in your arms,
Your love lifted me from the pit of depression,
Transforming it into a platform of obsession for you,
It is not surprising why my spirit is rising, longing for Your presence,
Lord, Lord, I want more,
I love Your embrace of grace,
Your sweet kiss of mercy and Your touch of kindness,
It is a collage of Your love,
Lord, You love me like no organism could,
When Jesus given His life on a cross made of wood,
I am free because what Your Word says in John 3:16,
You so love me,
That you gave me a chance to reconnect with Thee,
I seek Thee, oh, I seek Thee,
Your thoughts are toward me,
With a pattern so fatherly,
Your sweet love covers a multitude of my sins,
You are more than a friend,
Oh sweet Lord, the One whom I adore,
Who can escape Your allure?
When You open the door to restore,

You speak to my heart to jumpstart my adoration,
This river that flows from my eyes cries holy!
I long to be at Your feet, to lay on Your chest, and hear Your heartbeat,
It is easy to be intimate with Thee, because you so love me.

Words from My Belly Devotional

You Love Me

Scripture: John 3:16: "For GOD so loved the world that HE gave HIS only begotten son, so whoever believe in Him shall not perish but have eternal life."

Testimony

I was inspired to write this poem when I was sitting at the computer just reflecting on the goodness of the Lord. After that, I was overwhelmed with gratitude toward the Father and the Son. Just thinking of His love that graces not just me but all of us puts a smile on my face. God gives us chance after chance when really He could strike us down; He can do that because He is God. But because He is a God of unconditional love, He blesses us with Jesus so we can be close to Him, who created all things. You were created in love, you were blessed in love, you were corrected in love, you were given a second chance to receive eternal life in love. Receive His love by receiving Jesus, and even if you are saved and not in right standing with God, receive Jesus Christ once again. God loves you that much.

CHAPTER 2

Thoughts

THOUGHTS

Lord, I am just thinking, seeking answers to questions I had not asked. Is it my past or task that I have to perform? Is this the norm? What is normal? It is dressing formal for an occasion? Or is it dealing with situation after situation? Is there more to life than just living? Sitting on the rock of my purpose, my mind is demanding some sort of understanding. My Lord Jesus, you paid the ultimate price. The greatest sacrifice for people who are daily rolled the dice of their life. To be honest, I would have thought twice, but you are not me and that is a good thing. Still I wonder about my blunders. I know that You are God, and I am a child of yours—the blessings You have in store. Lord, you are taking me to the promised land; my destiny. I love you, Lord, because of who You are. You are my all and all, my bright and morning star.

Lord, I am just thinking,
Deeper in love with You I am sinking,
To drown in Your loving arms,
Where I am safe from all harm,
You are ever loving and judging,
My God, you show mercy upon me even when I was wrong,
When I was at my weakest,
You touch me like Samson and made me strong,
The more I think of Your goodness and Your grace,
It is easy for You to be in my heart where You have a place,
I am not worthy or deserving of Your kindness and Your tender mercies,
I just want to be in Your presence to pay homage to Thee,
Thank You, Jesus, for paying the cost,
You will always be in my thoughts.

Words from My Belly Devotional

Thoughts

Scripture: Proverbs 3:5–6: "Trust in the LORD with all your heart, and do not rely on your own understanding; think about HIM in all your ways, and HE will guide you on the right paths."

Testimony

Often I find myself pondering about my life. Where I come from? Who am I, and who am I in the Lord? What is my purpose for living on this side of heaven? I am sure that you have thought of these questions or have not given it any thought. The Word of the Lord says in Proverbs 3:5, "[D] o not rely on your own understanding." So I have to do the one of things that I have a problem of doing: stop thinking about it and start trusting God. Verse 6 says, "[T]hink about GOD in all your ways, and HE will guide you on the right path." So I mostly think about God and turn all my attention to Him; He starts speaking to me and tells me what to do and what to say and how to say it. Your thought should not be on the care of this life but on the One who can give you direction and affection.

Thoughts of a Righteous Writer

Who am I, let me hear it,
No, not flesh, I am spirit,
I occupy this vessel that my soul wrestles,
You might think I gifted,
But I am scripted,
By the Author and Finisher of my faith,
The One who gave strength to run this race,
Don't you know we are more beyond than what we see?
A people of purpose and destiny,
The Lord has been feeding and feeding me words,
A collection of nouns, adjectives, and verbs,
Pouring the blood of my pen on a canvas of white,
Praying that the words will give life,
And has the power of birth and insight,
The dormant soul,
Lo, I see my pen bleeding,
The blood spills on the white sheet,
Destroying the inner beast,
Defeat, let me repeat, defeat,
Which the serpent is,
With the Blood of the Christ we live,
I am not conforming to this world,
So they label me odd,
To those who have spiritual sense,
I am a writer, a child of God!

Words from My Belly Devotional

Thoughts of a Righteous Writer

Scripture: Jeremiah 1:4–5: "The word of the LORD came to me: I chose you before I formed you in the womb; I set you apart before you were born. I appointed you a prophet to the nations."

Testimony

This poem was born when I really knew what God called me to do through the gift of poetry. God planted seeds of talents or gifts in us before we existed in this reality. The wonderful thing was now I was gifted but gifted to glorify God and to encourage His people. What did He gift you with, and are you using it for His glory?

Spiritual Life Rhetoric

Eyes have not seen, nor ears have heard,
The verbs that are connected to your destiny,
Or understand your love for an unseen Being,
Which blood is freeing soul after soul,
From the pit far down below,
The Holy Spirit is telling you to walk on water like Peter,
But you worry about trouble tides and start to sink,
Renew your mind that is your thinking,
The rivers of wisdom from God is what you should be drinking,
Friends may come and friend may go,
But God's word never passes way,
So trouble won't last like yesterday,
No weapon formed against you shall proper this day,
As you sit there deep in thought,
Meditate on Jesus, who paid the cost,
Day to day and night after night you are on your knees,
Making know to the Father your supplications and pleads,
Asking Him to blot out every sin,
Repenting until there is no end,
You cry out in the midnight hour,
Lord, let your will be done!
And you are waiting for rely but there is none,
Patience is what God was teaching you,
Schooling to endure while you are going through,
The joy of the Lord is your strength,
Your noncarnal weapon is your defense,
Praise is a strong tool to win the battle,

To shake up the kingdom of darkness like a baby's rattle,
Surely, goodness and mercies shall follow you all the days of your life,
Through the joy and seemingly endless strife,
You have the victory, you should repeat it,
Because of the power of the blood of Christ; the devil is defeated,
Live like God wants you to live,
Victorious and with joy and faith,
Speak life to your situation; it is never too late,
The life you live is for Christ's sake,
Be encouraged and be strong through positive and all odds,
Just remember you are *a child of God*!

Words from My Belly Devotional

<u>Spiritual Life Rhetoric</u>

Scripture: 1 John 4:4: "You are from GOD, little children, and you have conquered them, because the One who is in you is greater than the one who is in the world."

Testimony

In this poem, I was led to touch upon a few spiritual issues that one might face in their walk with Jesus and encourage them to press on through scripture. Sometimes we need a reminder that we are children of the most high God. You can overcome anything because you serve a God who can do everything.

What Is so Merry about Christmas?

What is so merry about Christmas?
If you would ask me that question,
Then my mind will correlate my thoughts into an expression,
An expression of joy that is erupting in my being,
Like a volcano freeing gratitude,
The celestial seed that was planted in a chosen vessel,
So I don't have to wrestle with the plenty of death,
What so merry about Christmas?
It took Mary for me to be merry,
And a "Godsend" named Jesus who didn't tarry,
As I am thinking, rewinding the tape of my memories,
Of a holiday that has purpose and fill with destiny,
Santa doesn't have a clause in the devil's contract,
That was destroyed with one selfless act,
Rudolf may have a red nose,
But it can't compare to the redness of the blood of Jesus that flows,
What is so merry about Christmas?
With the CD, DVD, HDTV, can't come close to what is in the B-I-B-L-E.
That tells the story of the love of the Holy Father saying, "I will give them victory,"
If I can free you from the sunglasses of this worldly view of Christmas,
And put on the spiritual glasses to see clearly to make your exodus,
What is so merry about Christmas?
If I can break it down to its lowest common denominator,
On this day, God has given us a Savior.

Words from My Belly Devotional

What Is so Merry about Christmas?

Scripture: Luke 2:11: "[T]oday a Savior, who is Messiah the LORD, was born for you in the city of David."

Testimony

I was led to write this poem because people, even Christians, get caught in the commercialism of this holiday, this holy day that was set aside to honor the gift that was sent by God the Father. The world celebrates this holiday we call Christmas with icons other than Jesus. Santa Claus didn't die on the cross for your sins. Rudolf the Red-Nosed Reindeer did not intercede on your behalf when Satan accused you. Frosty the Snowman did not send the Holy Spirit to guide you on your life's journey. I encourage you to put "Christ" back in "Christmas."

CHAPTER 3

Wisdom

WISDOM

Wondering, wondering,
My thoughts drifting aimlessly or trying to find a target that is not seen,
My search continues without end,
Pondering, pondering, leaning on my own understanding,
My brain is demanding answers,
To questions that haunts my mental,
I need to know how and I need to know why,
Is there a procedure or guideless,
My oh my!
I am empty,
My mind is hungry and thirsty,
I need wisdom,
The very thing you can't get enough of,
It is continuous like a ring,
An endless circle going around and around; infinity,
King Solomon asked God for wisdom,
The reading of Proverbs with "verb" for action,
The attraction is knowing and showing,
Wisdom transcends time,
Evolving, growing like a flower in the field of the mind,
I have found my guidelines in the Bible,
Or Better Information Bringing Life Eternally,
In Hosea 4:6, "My people are destroyed for lack of knowledge,"
In my revelation, not knowing is not growing,
I must water the field of my mind and spirit with the waters of God's knowledge,
That the good fruit will bloom within me,

There is a destiny,
Starting the snowball effect of curiosity,
A curiosity about the Trinity,
God, the Son, and the Holy Spirit that dwell within me,
Wisdom is a precious woman like Solomon said,
I just want to sit at God's feet and be spiritually fed.

Words from My Belly Devotional

Wisdom

Scripture: Proverbs 3:13: "Happy is a man who finds wisdom and who acquires understanding."

Testimony

Wisdom is something I desire in a natural and spiritual sense. There is something about receiving wisdom from God through the Holy Spirit. The main source of tangible wisdom on this earth is the Bible. When you receive Christ into your heart, the Bible becomes more than a history book. It becomes a book of instruction for our everyday living.

Knowledge 4 Kingdom

Pardon me if you would allow me to pour water of knowledge on the garden of your mind to bear fruit. If knowledge is the key, then the success doors we want to walk into cannot be opened. I know, I know, knowledge is not fun; you'd rather have a gun or shake your bun in a video. Wait, wait, but hear me though. The best bet is what is in the text. So you won't be vexed during tests. You might find it boring; I can almost hear you snoring. You want to deal but here what is real. Fast cash won't last but knowledge is forever, let's put two and two together. 2 learn is equal 2 succeeding multiply by ABC and 123 with the sum of a college degree. You won't be a fish out of water and won't say, "Welcome to McDonald's, may I take your order?" With passion, you will build bridges and cross borders. You are not Generation X; you will be the generation next to pick up a check without worrying about debt. Learn what you can while you are young, and don't listen to those who tell you are dumb. You are fearfully and wonderfully made with God as your Creator; you can stand in these evil days. Now that you have your degree, that is one battle won. Now you can take your knowledge to advance the Kingdom. With integrity and grace plus a spray of the blood of Jesus in the devil's eyes like mace. Study and show yourself approved unto God. You are unique; to the world's eyes, you are odd. The haters, you don't have to fear them. Just receive knowledge 4 the kingdom.

Words from My Belly **Devotional**

Knowledge 4 Kingdom

Scripture: 2 Chronicles 1:10: "[G]rant me wisdom and knowledge so that I may lead these people, for who can judge this great people of YOURS?"

Testimony

There is a saying in Luke 12:48: "But the one who did not know and did things deserving of blows will be beaten lightly. Much will be required of everyone who been given much. And even more will be expected of the one who has been entrusted with more." If God entrusts you with something, He wants to you activate it for the Kingdom of God. You pray for it and now you are responsible for it. Be obedient; walk out in purpose through your gift that is great because it comes from the Lord.

INSIGHT

Restoring the way things are to the way things used to be. Lord, what are You saying? I am paying attention, what was that redemption? Those who have clean hands and a repenting heart can start. Lord, please grant me some clarity. Unity of the spirit . . . what? Lord, please take the wax out of my spiritual ears so I can hear. Thinking . . . thinking, oh my, I am leaning on my own understanding. Renew my mind so I can observe Your ways and follow Your laws. My back, I can almost feel the demons, trying to pull me backward instead of forward. One word, Lord, one word, I am listening for Your one word . . . huh? You said, "Free"; are my ears deceiving me? Sitting here on this chair, waiting for a word to declare. Time is not on my side, because I am bound by the minute and second hands of man's life span . . . thoughts. With an outstretched mental hand; my thought is reaching for clarity so I can understand the plan of the celestial man. Wondering, pondering the ways of the Father up above. Of increasing love like the dove from Noah that brought back a twig that signified the land that was promised is near. My soul set sail on the sea of simplicity connected and guided by the wind of God's breath. My thoughts are collaborating to form a revelation, but without the Holy Spirit, there is no graduation . . . mmm, there goes the miseducation. Hear ye, hear ye, all ye people that have been rounded up in the stable. Don't you know God is able? Able to carry you through the weather, put your hands together. The Lord is so clever. The tears of the night are replaced with joy in the morning. I am drifting, drifting, kissing the Master's feet with my praise and worship. The nakedness of my outpouring leaves me exposed for the world to see; what the world thinks doesn't bother me, I am free! I do not hate the player, but I hate the games the world plays when they are pawns in the dark side of the spiritual chessboard, praying that they are not checkmated. O my soul, where does it go? It has already been debated and won by the blood of Jesus that is concentrated. Daily, my knees are bruised by being between the porch and the altar so I can alter the plans of the enemy who is trying to hinder me and those who are connected to me from what had been ordained, our destiny. I am living in the land of free; there are some who eluded the "one nation under God." What god are you referring to? Is it the one who is telling you to oppress, depress, turning my brown eyes blue, or is it the One who sent His Son to die on the cross when it should have been you? O say, can you see the plot of our worse enemy, the mirror's imagery? That is the self, giving into the voice of falsehood, so we can burn like him in the "lake of fire" like wood. My doors are shut, slammed in the face of the enemy who tries to invade my inner space. No vacancy for the demon's hypocrisy in this vessel you see. On this day which the Lord has made, this wisdom that the Lord had laid for me to convey is, in your walk, be not afraid.

Words from My Belly Devotional

Insight

Scripture: 1 Corinthians 14:33: "For GOD is not the author of confusion but of peace, as in all churches of the saints."

Testimony

In this moment in time, I was letting my mind drift upward toward God. I was waiting for Him to talk to me. I came to Him expecting a word that will satisfy my understanding. As I sat there waiting at the computer, He began to pour into me. I was typing what I heard and then my understanding was open. How many times have you sat there and waited for the Lord to pour into you? Remember, a still cup gets filled quicker than a moving one.

CHAPTER 4

Storm

Ms. Temptress I. Lust

Since I cast you out from another, you have been a bother. You have been seeking to torment me and derail me from my destiny. Everyone has a demon; I guess you are mine. Unclean spirit from hell who chose to clothe yourself as a female. Your eyes burns right through me. Like a forest fire igniting thoughts of sinful desire. Your pouting lips, soft like cotton. From Monday to Sunday, you are trying to make me weak. Your voice is like the songs of the sirens, you are attempting to draw me near. Your skin smooth like a marble floor. The shape of your body seems perfect, as Michelangelo's great work. When you walk into the room, everything seems to stop; it seems as though you are walking in slow motion. Like a ghost, you haunt my dreams. Like a hungry lion to its prey, you are ready to pounce. How can I save myself for marriage when you are around? My flesh gets excited with the mere thought of you! *No!* I rebuke it out of my mind! Ms. Temptress I. Lust distracts me; I am almost at the point of frustration. Somebody exorcise this demon from my mind! This demon called Ms. Temptress I. Lust. Tormentor of my soul, ghost of my dreams. Lord, have mercy on me! I will resist you with all my being and you will see! The shackle of lust has no hold on me, I am free!

Words from My Belly Devotional

Ms. Temptress I. Lust

Scripture: 1 Corinthians 10:13: "No temptation has overtaken you expect what is common to humanity. GOD is faithful and He will not allow you to be tempted beyond what you are able, but with the temptation He will also provide a way of escape, so that you are able to bear it."

Testimony

I wrote this poem when I made a vow to God to abstain from sex until I am married. I had sex before, but when I took my walk with Jesus seriously, I stopped having sex. This was not an easy thing to do especially when you had a taste of it. The temptress was my lust for sex; in every turn I was tempted, in dreams, at work, and just being outside in my travels. I came so close to having sex, but the woman I was with said, "I would have sex with you, but I know you are saving yourself." That was my way of escape provided by God. The woman knew my walk and commitment with God. After that, it didn't get any easier. The enemy started to mess with my mind, putting thoughts and I was entertaining them. That was the trick: not to entertain them. So when I focused on Jesus and the mission that He has me on, it got easier. True enough, moments of loneliness come and go, but with His strength, I was able to handle them. I held on little over 10 years until God presented me with my Rib, my Eve, my comparable Partner. There is nothing impossible for God: with the strength of the Lord, you can bear!

THE STORMS

I am floating on the sea of my life,
The gentle breeze of good times blows,
The sun shines bright on my future,
The seagulls are my friends, flying around me,
I am thinking to myself, how good it is,
Then the cloud of doubt covers my bright future,
The strong winds of bad times blew,
The seagulls crap on me, some friends,
Now I am thinking to myself, *What is happening?*
Big waves of despair crash upon me,
I can hear the thunder of doom above me,
Than the octopus of conflict pulls me down,
Someone please help me!
My faith is the only thing that is keeping from giving up,
Just when my body can't loosen its hold,
I swim to the surface,
The thunder of doom was silenced,
The waves of despair stopped,
The seagulls left,
The cloud of doubt was cleared,
The storm is over.

Words from My Belly Devotional

The Storm

Scripture: Mark 4:37–39: "A fierce windstorm arose, and the waves were breaking over the boat, so that the boat was ready being swamped. But HE was in stern sleeping on the cushion. So they woke HIM up and said to HIM, 'Teacher! Don't you care that we're going to die?' HE got up, rebuked the wind, and said to the sea, 'Silence! Be still!' The wind ceased, and there was a great calm."

Testimony

At this point in time, I was on a roll with Jesus and doing God's will. All of a sudden, all Hades broke loose. It felt like a storm was raging in my life. Just like the disciples, I cried out to the Lord to calm my storm. I didn't receive an immediate response like them. I have to be in this storm for a reason. Until I got that revelation, that's when the storm cleared in my life. You can't effectively minister to someone unless you've been through a storm. Let me add this in: you can minister to someone after you've been through a storm, not while you're in one.

Peace of Mind

If you only knew,
What goes on in my mind,
If you were able to read my thoughts,
You will find out that I am a tormented soul,
Every day, I am fighting myself,
Trying to do right,
Living the life,
Day and night,
Fighting the continuous fight,
The ring is my mind,
In this corner you have God,
In the other corner is the devil,
In the middle is myself,
The rounds are unlimited,
The fight gets tiresome,
At times I want to give up!
I am tired of saving myself for marriage!
I am tired of being Mr. Goody Two-Shoes!
I am tired of holding my tongue!
I want to cuss so bad, I could scream!
I am on the edge of insanity!
Look into my eyes and tell me what you see!
I am alone, tired, and frustrated!
At night, I break down and cry!
Asking God why, why!
He said to me,
Dry those tears from your eyes,

I really do care,
I will never give you more than you can bear,
I heard your cries and shouts,
I will never leave you without a way out,
Don't worry any longer,
After you get through this you will get stronger,
I thank You, Lord, I can get through it!
With you, I know I can do it!
Everything will soon be fine,
Thank you, Lord, for this peace of mind.

Words from My Belly Devotional

Peace of Mind

Scripture: Romans 7:23: "But I see a different law in the parts of the body, waging war against the law of my mind and taking me prisoner to the law of sin in the parts of my body."

Testimony

Everyone has days of total confusion, when it feels like you are drowning in the issues of life and your mind is about to explode into nothingness. But thanks to God, He will bring you peace in the midst of it all. Just focus on Him. It may seem hard at first but it is not impossible. How bad do you want peace? If you want it, go to the One who will give it to you: Jesus.

EXECUTIONER

I see a man,
He is beaten up and bloody,
Then I see another person with a hooded mask,
The one with the hooded mask is the executioner,
He seems dark like my worst nightmare,
I am thinking to myself, *Why must the good ones die?*
He has three nails and a hammer,
The first nail, the nail of ungodliness,
Bang! The pain!
The second nail, the nail of faithlessness,
Bang! The horror!
The third nail, the nail of lust of the world,
Bang!
I vomited at the sight of it all,
Out of frustration, I yelled, "Enough!"
I ran, tackled the executioner!
I ripped off the hooded mask,
I paused, the executioner was me, it was me!
I am the one who backslid!
What have I done! What I have I done!
Lord, please forgive me!
Please forgive me!

Words from My Belly Devotional

Executioner

Scripture: Acts 4:10: "[L]et it be known to all of you and to all the people of Israel, that by the name of JESUS Christ the Nazarene-whom you crucified . . ."

Testimony

When I wrote this poem, I was thinking about the death of Jesus. It was because of me and my sinful nature that He died on the cross. I might as well be the one hammering the nail in Him and stabbing Him on His right side. I know He didn't just die for me but for all of us. I felt so bad, but it made me realize that God loves me and I have so much to live, die, and rise up for so I can come back to God clean.

A Good Man's Dilemma

I am walking a thin line between good and bad,
Should I pick the fruit from the tree of knowledge?
Or leave it alone like God told me,
Temptation flocks to me like a bunch of moths to a flame,
They try to claim me like a trophy,
To me, sex is like the flu; it is contagious,
A good man's dilemma winner or sinner,
It's not easy to be single and saved,
Life is a test; you pass or fail,
Here on earth, between heaven and hell,
I live this life for Christ,
Who gave his life for me so hell won't be my destiny,
I try to be Superman, but like Superman, I have a weakness,
My flesh; I can't be free from it,
Because it is a part of me,
A good man's dilemma: winner or sinner,
It is easy to do wrong and hard to do right,
The continuous battle of good and evil in my mind,
It's giving me a headache day and night,
I want to give up like an outgunned thief,
But my faith won't accept defeat,
Jesus watches over me while He sits on the right seat,
A good man's dilemma: winner or sinner,
At times it feels like the devil is eating my righteousness for dinner,
How long will my heart last?
My flesh keeps writing a check that my soul can't cash,

Take a look at the movie of my life,
Now showing: a drama, a good man's dilemma,
But this movie has a happy ending with God getting the credit,
A good man's dilemma: winner or sinner—winner!

Words from My Belly Devotional

A Good Man's Dilemma

Scripture: Ephesians 6:12: "For our battle is not against flesh and blood, but against the rulers, against the authorizes, against the world powers of darkness, against the spiritual forces of evil in the heavens."

Testimony

For a time I was wrestling against my flesh, but I was wrestling against a perverse spirit. That spirit used to torment me day and night. It was to a point where I thought I was crazy. It already knows I was saving myself for marriage and I had sex before. TV and radio did not help at all because it promotes sex. When I set my mind on God and His love and realize the authority He had given me, I was able to resist that spirit. Having the full armor of God helps.

Masquerade

Every is a Masquerade,
Individuals wearing a mask it's like a huge parade,
These collections of false impression,
Leads me to ask the question,
What mask am I wearing?
In the mirror, I am staring at a face whose race is black,
It is a mask: who am I really?
So many questions, it stacks up to the ceiling,
Am I a mixture of tissues, organs and bones?
The earth where it manifested; its home,
It is mask; every day, it is a graduation,
From my emotion when I smile,
When I don't want to be in some people's location,
Thank God for being saved,
If I was to act out what I feel,
Some people will not see another day,
Lord, please help me!
Grant me the strength to overcome this mask,
Who is trying to dictate my destiny,
For a little over a quarter century,
The mask has been plaguing me,
Slowly the mask is coming loose,
No more will this mask hide the truth,
When it is time for the great sleep,
The mask will be the only thing that is deceased,
The mask does not wear me; I wear it,
The mask is flesh but I am spirit,

No more will it hide, the light that abides,
In me to set me free,
Time after time I count the costs,
It is time to take this mask off,
When I see my heavenly Father,
What a great and glorious day,
I will have no regrets,
Because I chose not to live my mortal life in a masquerade.

Words from My Belly Devotional

Masquerade

Scripture: James 1:23–24: "Because if anyone is a hearer of the word and not a doer, he is like a man looking at his own face in a mirror; for he looks at himself, goes away, and right away forgets what kind of man he was."

Testimony

In this poem, I used a mask as a metaphor for my flesh and issues. The outer part of me is not the real me, but my spirit who dwells in me is the real me. Often we mask who we are in Christ. When we conform to this world, we put on the mask; when we sin and don't live up to our Christian mandate, we put on the mask. From the outside looking in, we look like the world instead of Jesus Christ. Let's shed off this earthly mask and show our real faces: the face of Jesus who dwells in our hearts.

In Line, Out of Line

I am following a straight glowing road. It is the path that God has laid out just for me to follow. Like elementary school math, I thought this path was easy. Being ignorant, I let ungodly things catch my attention like a flyball in the infield. Then, the glowing road started to dim because of my disobedience and sin. Down toward the valley of the shadows of death, on the road of uncertainty. This road is foggy, twisted, and rough.

Lord, please forgive me,
I have gone astray,
Now my future is cloudy and gray,
Lord, show me the way back to path,
I know I have messed up,
Please don't laugh,
I want to go back in line,
Back to the glowing path,
So bright and sublime,
The quickest way from A to B,
Is a straight line,
I know that now and I can see,
It is so bright; my destiny,
I feel my heavenly Father's energy,
I am back on the straight line,
Focus on soul, body, and mind,
I do not want to be out of line,
I know full well I don't have the time,
To use, abuse, subdued, allude,
And mess around with fools,

How long can I be on the straight and narrow?
Sin going to shoot me like an arrow,
Satan, why do you tempt me so?
Tempting me with shortcuts,
Distracting me from where I have to go,
I am walking this line!
I might get out of line!
But I am getting back in line!
I want what the Lord has for me!
It's in His will, in my destiny!
The devil can knock me down time after time!
But I refuse to get out of line!

Words from My Belly Devotional

In Line, Out of Line

Scripture: Matthew 7:13–14: "Enter through the narrow gate. For the gate is wide and the road is broad that leads to destruction, and there are many who go through it. How narrow is the gate and difficult the road that leads to life, and few find it."

Testimony

This poem illustrates my walk when I was first saved. I thought it would be easy, you know the usual: living right, go to church, and be active in church. I thought that was walking with Christ. It was a lot more was I supposed to do than just that. When trouble set up my life, that didn't help me. I needed a relationship with Jesus; going to church was fine, but you need a personal relationship with Jesus, who bled and died for you and me. As soon as I realized that, I went to the Father because I knew I was off and needed to get it right with Him. I could not handle this road I was in. After I got it right with Him and asked Jesus to come into my heart, I was placed back on the right path toward my destiny. It may be rough at times, but I have Jesus as my travel partner.

THE WORLD'S REJECT

In looking at me, I am an outcast for the world's normalcy,
A nomad walking this planet, whose thinking is not a worldview,
But a view through a celestial being's eyes who truly loves you,
I am the world's reject because I reject it and its way,
I'm trying to speak the gospel of truth before the end of the last day,
The world views me as the freak from the norm,
I am cast out of the popular lifestyle that will eventually have them torn,
Verbal stones the world throws at me from the gates,
I don't mind as long as I speak the living truth for my Father's sake,
Staring at me, tearing at me, and sometimes branding me,
Because of my belief,
Internal wounds scar my body,
But because of another strife I am healed,
To the world thinking it is surreal,
In the library of their thought pattern it is fiction,
But it is an autobiography of God's loving and restoring tradition,
I am still walking; the world's rejected and neglected,
However, that doesn't really bother me because I am God-accepted,
Go on and look at me with eyes rolled back in your head,
Turn your back on me and wish me dead,
I shall live and not die,
When Jesus arise, I rise,
Rise above the carnal thinking that keeps people sinking,
Deeper into the quicksand of the devil's plan to destroy man,
I am still walking and walking, step by step,
I am a servant of God, the world's reject.

Words from My Belly **Devotional**

The World's Reject

Scripture: Luke 21:16–17: "You will even be betrayed by parents, brothers, relatives and friends. They will kill some of you. You will be hated by everyone because of My name."

Testimony

It is not easy being a Christian. It is bad enough you are trying to live right, but the world or those who don't know Christ do not like your lifestyle. The world encourages having sex as much as you want as long as you have a condom, but you are saving yourself for marriage. The world doesn't understand the Christian lifestyle because we are not of the world. Often someone will reject something that they don't understand. So the world rejects Jesus, the one who came to save it. So I encourage you to press on no matter what comes. Hold on to your confession, for it is better to live for things eternal than for things that are temporary.

Do You Know Me?

If I were to stand before you who are called redeemed,
Would you understand my inner man?
When I stand before you, do you see a question mark?
I see knives in front of me,
I am afraid to turn around because in my back they may impale me,
With a verbal sword you cut me and left me bleeding,
Where is my healing?
Excuse me; this is what I am feeling,
You came with correction,
I received admonishment but you wrapped it not in love but objection,
I was left praying to heal the wounds,
That left my emotion entombed,
It is apparent you don't know me like you should,
If you did, you would have not cut me like wood,
If God can forgive me, I can forgive you,
As a child of God I must try to get to know you,
And ultimately love you.

Words from My Belly Devotional

Do You Know Me?

Scripture: Mark 11:25: "And whenever you stand praying, if you have anything against anyone, forgive him, so that your Father in heaven will also forgive you your wrongdoing."

Testimony

This poem is combination of church hurt. The hurt came from church leaders. If it was from a member, I would have handled it well, but this came from the ones who are supposed to be spiritual, the ones who are supposed to give the heart of God. Have to ever looked up to one of your church leaders? They seem so perfect, the way that the Lord uses them, and they speak words of wisdom. However, I forgot the one most important thing: *they are human*. My heroes turn into zero before my eyes when they wear masks. It was a hard pill to swallow, but the Bible says to forgive them. That is the hardest thing to do, to forgive, because you can't forget what they have done to you, especially if it is someone you loved and admired. It took me a while, but I forgave them and moved on with my life so that God can use me. I pray that you forgive whoever hurt you so that you can move on. No one knows you totally but God.

Looking 4 You

Come out, come out, Lord, wherever you are,
I need You now but You seem far,
My soul is sunk in deep despair,
I'm trying to crawl out, trying to get some air,
Deeper and deeper down the pit of worries,
I wonder and ponder if you hear me,
Do you feel me?
Lord, where are You!
Do You hear my cries?
Your Word said You never leave my side!
I am looking for You like lose keys,
You are the key to free me,
I am trying not to be deceived because You are not mock,
But this fire I am in is too hot,
Where are You?
I loved You!
I had served You!
I was laughed at for You!
I am crying like a frustrated baby,
Did I do something wrong? Hmm, maybe,
Lord!
"My son, I am here,
I am always near,
You had your ears clogged with worries,
I was calling you buy you didn't hear Me,
I was there when you cried yourself to sleep,
I was there when you were on the edge of hell's seat,

I was there,
I care,"
Looking for You to hear from You is all I wanted,
I am sorry for focusing on myself and having my soul haunted,
I can hear You now and still, that's what I'm going to do,
You were near when I was looking for You.

Words from My Belly Devotional

Looking 4 You

Scripture: Psalm 22:11: "Do not be far from me, because distress in near and there is no one to help."

Testimony

I was at a low point in a way. It seemed that the whole world was against me and God had left me. I was so worried about myself and the problem I was facing; when I prayed to God, I didn't receive an answer because I didn't look for God with my heart. That is why it seems God was not there because I was searching for Him the wrong way.

Testimony of a Nice Guy

God made me a male,
I should thank him for that,
I am tall in length, slim in width; eyes brown,
I am an endangered breed, a nice guy,
Being a nice guy is hard,
My mother and father made me this way and the grace of God,
Can you handle being in a relationship with a nice guy?
When I am open and honest, can you handle the truth?
When I pay attention to you, can you handle the
spotlight or you tell me to leave you alone,
When I am extra nice to you, do you think I am hiding something?
When a better-looking man comes around, you treat me like a dead leaf,
Left blowing in the wind,
All I can do is pick up my heart that was crushed
by your three-inch heel and move on,
Why were you with me?
Is it what I can give you, or is it that I will
never leave you like a faithful dog?
In the earthly realm, nice guys finish last,
I am beginning to believe that,
I may have friends and a social life,
But I feel alone,
But if I slap you down!
If I sleep with your sister, cousins, and your best friend!
If I lie and pay no attention to you, I guess I am a boyfriend then!
It's morning, open your eyes!
When your body is aching, I gave you a rubdown!

When you had a bad day, I made you smile!
I am your best friend, your lover, and that shoulder to cry on!
I treated you like the beautiful queen you are!
But I guess you can't handle that!
Lord, release me from this troublesome pain!
Alone, heartbroken, frustrated!
Nice guys finish last, nice guys finish last, I wish this feeling would pass!
Just when I thought all hope was lost,
This experience propelled me to the cross,
Let me tell you this because this is real,
The emotional wound I had is now healed,
Hear me because this is true,
I can look you in the eyes and say I forgive you,
Look at me now with my head held high,
Giving you a testimony of a nice guy.

Words from My Belly Devotional

Testimony of a Nice Guy

Scripture: Colossians 3:13: "[A]ccepting one another and forgiving one another if anyone has a complaint against another. Just as the Lord has forgiven you, so also you must forgive."

Testimony

Everybody wants to be loved. My parents raised me the best way they could: they dragged me to church and in every church event and function there was; I was raised in humble beginnings. A lot of that shaped a part of who I am. I knew how to treat a lady. This poem is about the relationships I had. I wanted so bad to be loved by another, I dealt with loneliness; that is one of the factors that led me to the wrong woman. I treated all these women like queens, but they can't seem to handle that I am really a nice guy or they think I am weak. In my mind, do they want a guy slapping them around, calling out their name, and treating them like dirt? I was a little confused. But this is all about forgiveness and being healed for the love that God picked for me. If I did not forgive those women who hurt me, I would have brought that hurt into my marriage. It would not be fair to her. If you have exes, x them out of your heart by forgiving them so you have a wonderful relationship with your other and with God.

CHAPTER 5

Warfare

INTERCEDE

Glorious Lord, here I am between reality and eternity, seeking your face. In your presence, there is fullness and holiness. Lord, I am on my knees because there is nothing higher than You. I kneel in awe of You. Your radiant light is so bright that it chases away the darkness of fear, the cloud of doubt, and the shadow of impurity. You are so holy; You are the one that molded me. Lord, I am here not only to praise you but to intercede. There are a lot of Your children who needs to be free. There are those who don't know their purpose and destiny. I know You hear the moaning and wails; Lord, let the blood of Jesus prevail! Lord, protect our coming out and going in, Lord have mercy for we have sinned, with Jesus there is not a friend like Him. Lord, grace us until our expected end. Lord, let your will be done in our lives, to our children, husbands, and wives. Take us to next walk with You; we don't know how to reach it, in our carnal minds we don't know what to do. Holy Spirit, on this day, have your way. Lord, do what You have to do! Lord, as long as You move. Move by Your power, move by Your grace! Lord, please move in this place! If it is home, work, school, church, or play! Father, I implore You, please manifest today! Life is short, and we as Your children can't afford to miss Your shift. Place us, Lord, and sign it with Your anointed kiss. Free those who are in bondage. Master, you called us and it is a privilege. Take us there, into the unknown portals of Your love. Father! I plead the blood! I plead the blood over every situation, large or small! I owe nothing to the devil because Jesus paid it all! With the fruit of my lips I spread your fame, this I pray in Jesus's name, amen.

Words from My Belly **Devotional**

<u>Intercede</u>

Scripture: 1 Thessalonians 5:18: "Pray constantly."

Testimony

The Word of God tells us to pray. I don't know about you, but praying with faith can change things. That is why it is important that we pray for one another. I find it comforting to know that someone out there is praying for me. Pray for your family, church, community, city, state, country, and the world. You never know what is going to happen if you don't pray. I encourage you pray and seek the Lord with faith and the knowledge that He will hear you. Your prayers can change things!

360 Degrees

Would it be fine if I could speak my mind or tell you what is on my heart or if you want to hear my spirit? My eyes—two natural, one spiritual—looks upon this lifetime. The seeds of my generation fall on the concrete with a lack of soil to cover them. My question is when did reality TV and BET receive a master's degree in life-ology? The gardener called TV implanted seeds in our seeds, what to do, and what to say, and implying it is okay to lay before their wedding day. As the saying goes, you sleep with dogs, skirt, or pant, you will wake up with fleas or in this day in age, STDs like HIV. Lord, I am on my knees asking where did we go as a community, family, and ministry made a left turn while on the road of spiritual integrity. Excuse me, Father, if you would allow me to intercede on my knees between the porch and the altar. Forgive us; we have faltered. Lord, this time we are not singing the same old song plus not sticking our noses where they don't belong but to be right standing with You. It is funny how we do this 360 degrees with Thee. We start with Thee, we fall until we hit bottom, repent, and climb back to You. On this merry-go-round of ups and downs and round and around, Lord, please stop the ride when we come full circle.

Words from My Belly **Devotional**

360 Degrees

Scripture: Romans 12:2: "Do not be conformed to this age, but be transformed by the renewing of your mind, so that you may discern what is the good, pleasing, and perfect will of GOD."

Testimony

Too long the influences of this world have people in their grip. The TV programs of today send messages, saying that it is okay to do this and that, which is opposite of what the Bible says. I wonder sometimes if we as a body are letting the TV raise our children and ourselves. Are we allowing what we see dictate how we are supposed to act? Even though there are good programs, they are nothing compared to the program that God has for us. Turn from this world and turn to God through Christ Jesus.

His Armor

If no weapon formed against me shall prosper, if the Lord is for me and He is more than the world against me, whom shall I fear? Excuse me if I shed a tear because my doubting thoughts have left me opened. Doubt has turned my shield of faith into the size of a plate. Being absentminded, I forgot to put on the helmet of salvation, to protect my head from words of dread. Please don't find it odd that my feet are not shod, ready to preach the gospel of peace. Uncertainty left my legs a little weak. As I recall, the Word said, with God's armor take it all. Realistically, I only put on the pieces that suit me when I should have the entire armory.

With this sword, which is the Word of God, I shall stab and grab what belongs to me. Truth is around me, salvation on my head, and I wear the breastplate of righteousness to protect my heart that is Spirit-led. With my trust strengthened, my faith shield has enlarged, plus my feet are ready to charge, to spread the gospel of peace so the body of Christ can increase.

With bruised knees, I will pray for the saints for all occasions,
To destroy the spirit of persuasion,
To help further ourselves to that spiritual graduation,
Trials and tests may come with overwhelming odds,
But I can stand against them with the armor of God.

Words from My Belly Devotional

His Armor

Scripture: Ephesians 6:11: "Put on the full armor of GOD so that you can stand against the rulers, against the authorities, against the world powers of darkness, against the spiritual forces of evil in the heavens."

Testimony

If you are a child of God, if you accepted the Lord Jesus Christ, you are public enemy number one in Satan's eyes. It is bad enough that you are at war with yourself, but Satan wants to add more grief. That is why it is important to have truth, righteousness, faith, salvation, the Word of God, and the will to tell others about the gospel. These are the armor of God; you can't fight without all the pieces of the armor. You have to be protected in all areas of your life: your mind, body and soul. So take up your armor and fight the good fight of faith!

In the Fight

Into the belly of the beast I plunge,
With my sword I lunge,
Swing, slicing like a whirlwind of fury,
I fight through the darkness,
The darkness is all around me,
Surrounding me with despair,
This gets tiresome, this spiritual warfare,
I must fight on; there are too many souls at stake,
With my fighting I can't afford to faint,
Before Genesis, Satan has been my nemesis,
With scare tactics, I must not be startled,
My weapons of warfare are not carnal,
Personal demons I must fight through,
Thanks be to God who gave me the victory, I can't lose,
With my Father's armor and my prayers at hand,
Against the darkness, I can stand
With a light that burns bright fueled with my zeal,
The darkness will know I am for real,
For the glory of my God and His people at large,
I charge,
By God's strength, I can go on day and night,
He made me a warrior and I am in the Fight!

Words from My Belly Devotional

In the Fight

Scripture: 2 Timothy 4:7: "I have fought the good fight, I have finished the race, I have kept the faith."

Testimony

Sometimes you have to get down and dirty with the enemy. Too long he has been messing with you, your family, and your money. The Word of God says, "Greater is He that is within me than he that is in the world. God has given you power to trend over all the powers of the enemy. Take everything that loser has stolen from you and your family! Enough is enough; get back your peace, love, joy, children, husband, wife, business, dreams, goals, and money! You have the power through Jesus—use it!

TAKE YOUR HANDS OFF MY SPIRIT BABY!

There is a hand that is trying to rock my cradle,
These unclear hands is trying to put a demand,
On my baby that was not made by man,
Your words and hands are slippery as silk!
Your will not feed my baby with worldly breast milk!
Away with your lies and your gloom and doom!
This baby is not yours; it came out of my spiritual womb!
You think you know how to raise this child?
Back off before I get buck wild!
Your claim on this baby will not hold up in court!
His Daddy God pays all the child support!
Leave my baby alone!
You better have a relationship with God and have one of your own!
Child stealer, dream killer, and doubt filler!
This baby called ministry will live; why?
Because it won't lie!
I will tell once again, take your hands off my baby!
I might let you live, maybe!
Who died and made you nurse maid?
Were you there when there was a price to be paid?
I don't care if you are man, boy, girl, or lady!
Last warning: take your hands off my baby!

Words from My Belly Devotional

Take Your Hands off My Spiritual Baby!

Scripture: Revelation 12:4: "His tail swept away a third of the stars in heaven and hurled them to the earth. And the dragon stood in front of the woman who was about to give birth, so that when she did give birth he might devour her child."

Testimony

God has made you pregnant, whether you are male or female. He has placed inside of you ministries and gifting. You felt the pains of giving birth to your "spiritual child." However, no other than you have given birth to something special. The child is so special that they want a hand in it too. No one has the right to your ministry or gifting but God and those who are sent by God to help in not taking over your spirit child. The false ones will try to offer their opinion and ideas on what you should do when the Holy Spirit should guide you on how to make your baby that God trusted you and you alone with. Tell the others to back off—this is your baby, not theirs!

CHAPTER 6

For Her

WOMAN OF HIS WORTH

As my eyes look upon thee, I can't help but notice your radiant beauty. The Light that dwells within your heart enhances your natural presence. Like conjoined triplets, grace and mercy have attached themselves to you. What special clay did God use to create a treasure like you? A priceless vessel on the tables of the Father. Proverbs expresses, "Who can find a virtuous woman? For her price is far above rubies." Woman of His worth, standing in the doorway of reality and eternity. I speak life to thee, fruit of life. I speak love, joy, peace, long-suffering, gentleness, goodness, and faith. In the assembly, I behold you as you shed carnality and put on your priestly garment of praise. You labor before the Lord, being in awe of His presence. The price of you has already been paid by Jesus's blood; the price of you was too high for me to buy. You are like pure gold fresh from the fire, a diamond in the rough on this mortal coil. Woman of His worth with beauty and grace, continue to touch the hardened heart in this earthy place. The Light shines brightest when its dark. You can shine in the space where you are. What untold riches dwell in your spirit? What undiscovered fortunes await us in your heart? Your smile and your love are worth the world to me. If for a while, borrow my eyes to see you the way I see you. The beauty I see, I ask God to give me His vision and I beheld you and I see you perfect. What are you worth? Just like God priced you—the whole world.

Words from My Belly Devotional

Woman of His Worth

Scripture: Proverbs 31:10: "Who can a virtuous woman? For her price is far above rubies."

Testimony

Women are a gift. They are very special, and they have the ability to build you up or tear you down. A godly woman is the most precious of all. I find that godly women can go beyond the strength of normal woman's. When I wrote this poem, I was watching this godly woman who happened to be my spiritual mother, but she wasn't then. Over time, she loved me and nurtured me in all things God. It was a joy just being around her, and mind you, I was in my twenties. If you find a godly woman, connect yourself to her and learn from her, but make sure she is a godly woman because there are pretenders. If you find a true godly woman, you have found a treasure.

A Virtuous Scent

Before me stands a closet that is closed with a glow that is coming from the cracks. The door opens and there stands the silhouette of Eve. Her eyes are in awe, her mouth speechless; seemingly she is trying to catch her breath. As this seed bearer slowly walks past my person, an aroma captures my spiritual nostrils' attention. It was a familiar scent, flashbacking to the time I repented and was propelled to the throne room. That was the scent, the scent of the throne room. My eyes gazed in amazement of the woman's atmosphere changing the reality of the place that my feet tread upon. As she exited out of my vision, I smelled a foul stench of decay. On the floor by the closet were her rags of carnality dying. I look closely, her shirt of depression decomposing, the skirt of abuse rotting, her shoe of disobedience fading, and the belt of bondage lifeless. I turned from it and walked in the path of that woman, the virtuous scent was still present. The sweet smells of joy, peace, liberty, and faith fill the air. Where she comes from, where she went is my question; it does not matter, she has a virtuous scent.

Words from My Belly Devotional

<u>A Virtuous Scent</u>

Scripture: Song of Songs 4:10: "How delightful your love is, my sister, my bride. Your love is much better than wine, and the fragrance of your perfume than any balsam."

Testimony

It is a wonderful thing to see a woman deliver from bondage. Having bags and bags of issues make you look stinky. It is like you have sunk and no one wants to be around you. Having issues affects your mood and in turn affects those you love. When you are delivered from those things, it's like you have something new on and you smell good. Once you have the smell of God's love, mercy, grace, and freedom, people will be drawn close you, in turn making them smell good.

THOSE EYES

Through those eyes is what contains the truth about your spirit. If I were to gaze at your eyes, I would behold a garden of beauty. A spirit of love that has only been cultivated by the Father above. Your voice is what people hear, but those eyes is what I peer. What I see is a wonderful vessel ministering to God. A pure dove flying free in the heavens. The throne room scent is on you. Do you see what I see? A soul of love, kindness, and knowledge. Oh dove of this earth, I can't lock you in a cage in dominion of your gift. People need to understand it is a kiss to God wrapped in praise and worship. Don't mind me if you talk to me and I look away because I see beauty in those eyes. It's enough to make me shy. If people would sit at the gate of your temple and look in, the inner worship and adoration would change the trend of looking outwardly. Those eyes, a gateway to your soul, a wonder to be behold. You are wonderful, I had to write it; woman of God, I love your spirit!

Words from My Belly Devotional

<u>Those Eyes</u>

Scripture: Matthew 6:22: "The eye is the lamp of the body. If your eye is good, your whole body will be full of light."

Testimony

It is a funny thing: if I look into a person eyes, I can see who they are. Everybody has that ability. If you notice that a person can't look you in the eye, something is wrong or they did something they should not have done. In this poem, I was observing a praise and worship leader. Many people see her for her gift of singing when there is more to her than her vocal ability. I admit I have done the same thing until I talked to her and looked into her eyes. I saw more than what people perceive her to be. So from then on, I look at people beyond what they are able to do. I encourage you to do the same; you may find a treasure in an earthen vessel.

MISSING PIECE

There is a rib missing from my being. The void on my side is making me cry out to be whole. To be complete, I must meet the one who has been cultivated for me. Until that destined time, the Lord filled my insides. I pray for the day to draw near and peer into the eyes of my missing piece. For years, I denied myself the pleasure of another. Oh, the joy to have someone to love you back, to be in their embrace, and feel the warmth of tangible love. Upon that day, when God presents her to me, I can proclaim, bone of my bone and flesh of my flesh. I am holding fast to God's statement "It's not good for man to be alone," and with that, He has taken my bone and fashioned it to my Eve. For now, I cannot see the flower that was grown for me. One who is perfected and fire-tested for all weather. Still I wait for the date that is set aside for me to arise and behold her. I'll wait, can't say more or least, I will be waiting and serving my God, being patient, and being still for my love, my missing piece.

Words from My Belly Devotional

Missing Piece

Scripture: Genesis: 2:18: "Then the Lord GOD said, 'It is not good for the man to be alone.'"

Testimony

I don't know anyone who didn't want to be with somebody. I wrote this poem at a time I was saving myself for marriage. While I was saving myself, I knew within myself that I wanted to be with somebody. I know that God was creating that special woman just for me but I had to wait. While I was waiting, I was serving and He was working issues out within me. How can I be with someone if I have baggage? I would have brought that into the relationship, and speaking of relationships, I have to get my relationship with God right. It was worth it. He presented my missing piece, my wife, but God was my missing piece all along.

Gratitude to a Handmaiden

How can I put into words what your deeds already had spoken?
I am searching for adjectives to describe the person, place you are in,
I look unto the hills and behold your help,
I look down at the valley of your past trials,
Then I see the horizon of your future and it is bright,
Your voice is elegant with tone, like hitting the right note on a baby grand piano,
Playing a melody of integrity and encouragement,
When these two eyes look upon you, all I can see is grace, God's grace,
Our crossing was not by chance,
It was to feed off each other in this ministry called dance,
Oh, handmaiden who casts to the Father when you are heavily laden,
I know God has not forsaken,
God has given you the ability to maintain,
Through the hurts, through the pains, and even through the rain,
I speak joy where there is sorrow,
I speak hope for your tomorrow,
I speak health to your bones,
I speak God's love when you are alone,
I speak strength for the journey,
I pray the presence of God to fall on you when your heart is yearning,
This my small written expression of hope and gratitude,
My desire is for you to reach a better altitude.

Words from My Belly Devotional

<u>Gratitude to a Handmaiden</u>

Scripture: Luke 1:48: "[B]ecause He has looked with favor on the humble condition of His handmaiden. Surely, from now on all generations will call me blessed."

Testimony

I don't know if you've encountered a true servant of God. This woman, who is the inspiration of this poem, served the Lord's house with excellence. Her attitude, speech, and her doings in the church was one of grace. This woman servant wanted to do things right and surrounded herself with people who know what they are doing. She inspired me to be a good servant in the Lord's house and what I am called to do in the house of God. Look for a role model in church to propel you to be the best in what God wants you to do.

Anointed Songbird

Blessed ebony bird, your song is like candy,
Sweet to hear,
And like a voice in an empty room,
Your praises to God echo through the mind,
Your melody uplifts the troubled spirit,
Your passionate voice gives the weary soul strength,
God has blessed you with a gift,
And you use that gift for the glory of the Lord,
When you are not singing,
Your testimony is a harmony of hope,
When you lift up your hands,
It is a symphony of adoration,
Life will give you a broken wing,
And try to stop the song you sing,
That wing will heal and give you a new song,
How God rights what is wrong,
You inspired me, anointed songbird,
Through the singing and praises that I had heard,
Your voice is the hot fire that melts the cold heart,
And your faith is the enduring shield that stops the fiery darts,
You are more than just a voice,
You are God's choice,
May He wrap His arms around you like a ring,
Praise God, anointed songbird, and sing.

Words from My Belly Devotional

Anointed Songbird

Scripture: Psalm 149:1: "Hallelujah! Sing to the Lord a new song, His praise in the assembly of the godly."

Testimony

This was written to express my gratitude to a singer at church. Have you ever listened to an anointed singer? Their voice sounds angelic. I could come into the church with the worries of life, even those I should not have, and her voice would direct me toward the Heavenly Father. I thank God for praise and worship leaders because their duty is to usher you into the presence of God. They have to have a lifestyle of worship to be able to bring you into His Presence. They can't bring you into a place they have not been during the week. When you get a chance, thank that praise and worship leader who brought you into His presence. It is truly a gift to usher people into God's glory.

SPIRITUAL SIBLING

I am your brother: we have two different mothers, but we have the same heavenly Father. The One who guides and abides in us, so we can trust in the fact that He is there. You are my spiritual sibling birthed from the celestial womb of His glory. Now here is the story: in the beginning, you and I arrived in the gene pool of His holiness, to bless the earth and tell of His greatness. Through trail and trail and test, we connected at this appointed time to drop a fruitful dime. He assigned me to watch over you like a brother to a sister, but I am not your mister. I am not trying to get in between the sheets but to get between the porch and the altar so in God you can increase. Our souls intertwine like threads on a beautifully weaved tapestry called God's plan for our destiny, specially designed DNA to convey the wonder of His wisdom. I care for you and am willing to lay my life for you because no greater love than this for a man to lay down for a friend. I am your brother because we have the same Daddy. Our souls and hearts they complement, you are heaven sent, and your desire is to get into the holy tent. The Holiest of Holies where God can restore thee to fulfill your destiny. Once on the earth, but flying high to touch the sky, longing to reach the heavens to abide. Sister you are, brother I am and a friend. I am blessed and honored to be your kin.

Words from My Belly **Devotional**

Spiritual Sibling

Scripture: Matthew 12:50: "For whoever does the will of My Father in heaven, that person is My brother, sister and mother."

Testimony

There is nothing like having a spiritual sister. I'm talking about a person whom you can talk to on a spiritual level, and they are closer to you than your own siblings. Have you noticed that you spend more time with them on the phone and hanging out with them? I have many spiritual sisters, and they all help me through my journey with Christ. Now that I am married, my spiritual sister is my wife, who really have an inside knowledge of me. Your siblings in Christ are to bless you and bless you through.

Lover Flavors

Love, the highest form of emotion you feel toward another holy, is purely unconditional. Or is it purely lust? Often some guys get the two confused— one of the faults of being human. Sometimes thinking with the south and not the north. In the Civil War, the North won but in a personal civil war, the South gets the upper hand.

So ladies, if you are looking for a real man,
There is no such thing,
A man is a man,
Men are like ice cream,
There are different flavors,
Personality if you will,
There is tootie fruity,
He has issues, not sure of himself (sweet)
And there is rainbow,
He wants all flavors for himself (the player)
Now there is chocolate,
The most popular, most wanted, pleasing to the sight (the stud)
Whatever flavor you pick, don't pick Rocky Road,
Rocky is unstable and goes straight to your thighs,
So ladies, before you dip your spoon into your flavor,
Check the label, it might be no good,
Let the Creator of the ice cream serve you the flavor you need,
Don't get the flavor that pleases your senses
and brings you to your knees,

Before you go to the ice cream shop,
Taste and see that the Lord is good,
He will pick out the flavor of your life,
Two scoops of grace and mercy and a cherry on top for His Might.

Words from My Belly Devotional

Lover Flavors

Scripture: Matthew 26:41: "Stay awake and pray, so that you won't enter into temptation. The spirit is willing, but the flesh is weak."

Testimony

I wrote this poem to warn women about the temptation of looking for a man. As much as you want a man, you might make the wrong decision in choosing one. Oftentimes, the women I know make their decisions based on what the world says you should go after. They sometimes run after men when the Bible says, "He that finds a wife find a good thing." If you have a relationship with God, He will tell you if he is the one. Most of the time, God wants you to pursue a relationship with Him. He will love you so much because of the relationship you have with Him; He will prepare a man designed just for you. I encourage my sisters to seek the Man instead of seeking a man.

CHAPTER 7

4 Your Soul

My Third-Eye Rhetoric

This is from my third eye, my spiritual eye, so you can see,

This story of my past fallacies, shortcomings, and my steps toward victory,

Rewinding, I am burdened by chains, handcuffs, and shackles unseen by normal vision,

On my right hand, I have chains, each link stronger than the next,

With bipolar, religion, dyslexia, disobedience, to name a few,

On the left hand, I have handcuffs; I am handcuffed to the fence of ungodliness,

My feet are shackled with pride,

Question after question, I ask myself like I was a game show host,

Will I ever be set free?

Will someone get these restraints off me?

Is this my destiny?

There is no release I see,

Than a man of sorrow walk up to me and said,

"Ye of little faith with me you can make your escape,"

He touched my chains and said, "Deliverance,"

The chains fell off,

He touched my handcuffs and said, "Righteousness,"

The handcuffs popped open,

He touched my shackles and said, "Humility,"

The shackles fell down to the ground,

Then He said, "You were already freed, you just didn't believe,"

Mister, mister, how long will my righteousness last?

My flesh is writing a check my soul can't cash,

He said, "My Father, hear your cries and your calls and with My blood I paid it all,"

He said, "Don't you see, you are free, hell is no longer your destiny, you
have the victory,"
Free, victorious, how glorious,
If I am more than a conqueror,
Then these strongholds will fall down like the walls of Jericho,
With a complete praise like "seven,"
Now I am Holy Ghost filled and speaking in tongues,
But my spirit is numb from the hunger and thirst,
I am hoping that I can partake of the buffet of God's wisdom at church,
While I am absorbing all the preaching and teaching,
My personal trinity—mind, body, and spirit—are seeking answers,
To questions I never asked or had asked,
But the task is to wait like Job,
Behold, restoration finally arrived like graduation to a 12th grader,
I may be an outcast or cast out from the normalcy of this mortal coil,
I am able to put on a new garment not made by man,
I got to give God a handclap of praise,
Joy and praise revitalized, for that I am very much glad,
This rhetoric, this testimony is about God's grace and mercy I have.

Words from My Belly Devotional

My Third-Eye Rhetoric

Scripture: John 8:36: "Therefore if the Son sets you free, you really will be free."

Testimony

This poem is my salvation poem. I recognized that I was a sinner, and I have all these issues. I wanted to be free from it, and that is when I truly accepted Jesus into my heart. When I was young, I was baptized but did not have the understanding of what it means to accept the Lord and Savior Jesus Christ into your heart. When I accepted Him. I was free, and then I had questions about what I was experiencing. The hunger and thirst I have within me and what I must do. I was baptized for the second time because of my understanding of Jesus, and I made a recommitment. It is okay to make a recommitment, and there is nothing wrong in starting over. If you feel that you are not where you should be, make a recommitment to Jesus and be free.

The Box with My Name on It

I am walking down the aisle of the church,
I think there is a funeral going on,
Whose funeral, I don't know,
Slowly I make my way down the aisle,
I turn my head to the center column,
I see my family crying,
I am thinking to myself, it must be a family member who died,
For some reason, they didn't notice me,
As I approach the casket,
I see the mirror reflection; I see me,
Questions popped in my head,
How did this happen? When did it happen?
And most importantly, where am I going?
The penthouse or the basement?
I hear someone reading my obituary,
Note that they say the good things and not the bad things,
The soloist with beautiful music to sing,
Tears fall down the people's faces,
Some live near and some live in faraway places,
Cries and murmuring like a symphony echoes,
Why don't they just let me go?
Tears, shouting, cursing, and cries,
Please, my loved ones, get on with your lives,
It's over, this is it,
My flesh is laying in a box with my name on it.

Words from My Belly Devotional

The Box with My Name on It

Scripture: 1 Corinthians 15:31: "I affirm by the pride in you that I have in Christ Jesus our Lord: I die everyday!"

Testimony

Have you ever been overcome by your fleshly desires? As a believer in Christ, I believe it is very dangerous to be overcome by your flesh. I know that my fleshly desires will not be wiped out in a blink of an eye. I know it is a process; many of us don't like the word "process" because we live in a world where we have to have it here and now. Paul said, "I die every day"; I have to deny my wants and embrace God's will. I am not going to lie to you, it is hard, but the reward is worth it. God is not looking for strong or fast people, He is looking for people who can endure not just the worries of this life but also themselves. Once you decide in your mind that you will die daily, God will help you during the process.

SPIRITUAL ZOMBIE

I am the living dead; I die daily,
I deny my flesh its sexual desires,
I deny my flesh its evil intentions; I die daily,
I humble myself to those who have charged over me,
I think of others before I think of myself,
My pride I swallow; the taste gets nastier by the day,
And it gets harder to digest; I die daily,
I am shoveling dirt on my rotting flesh,
No good can come from it,
My spirit is doing the shoveling,
The more my flesh rots, the stronger my spirit gets,
I walk mindlessly on this rock,
Like the living dead,
I have this uncontrollable need to feed,
Feed my spirit knowledge, spirituality, and faith,
My flesh is slowly decomposing,
While my spirit is steady growing; I die daily,
My heart and flesh fails me,
But God is my strength and my portion,
Guiding my corpse in the right direction,
Walking slowly with my flesh dragging: I die daily,
My flesh, my flesh is dying,
While my spirit is shining,
What a great and glorious day when it dies,
Ashes to ashes, dust to dust,
Don't bury me with verbal dirt,
I am not dead yet; I am alive in Christ,

It's just my flesh that is decaying,
A lifeless shell with a strong power source inside,
I die daily, I die daily,
Nothing good can come from this flesh; it tends to fail me.

Words from My Belly Devotional

Spiritual Zombie

Scripture: Romans 6:11: "So, you too consider yourselves dead to sin, but alive to GOD in Christ Jesus."

Testimony

Merriam-Webster Dictionary defines "zombie" as a person who is believed to have died and been brought back to life without speech or free will. In this case, I am dead in sin but alive in Jesus Christ: a spiritual zombie. We are all in the flesh, but we are not flesh but spirit. Once we accept Jesus as Lord and Savior, the flesh dies and our spirit arises. I tell people I have a sports car spirit engine in a broken-down body. When I am with follow believers, it is the day and night of the living dead in Christ!

BIRTH OF MINISTRY

During my intimacy with God,
He impregnated me with the seed called ministry,
As the unseen fetus grows in my soul,
I travail with wails and moans,
Oh Lord, it hurts!
Is it time to give birth?
My patience rises and falls like the tide,
I wish I had some spiritual midwives,
My emotions are divided like fractions,
Oh, there goes another contraction,
Lord, this is frustrating,
Do I have to scream twice?
Where is my midwife?!
This hurts so bad I could curse,
Oh, I am about to give birth,
Here we go, 1, 2, 3,
Oh, how wonderful to see,
I'll name you Ministry; you look like your Daddy,
God has given you to me to run this race,
To go forth and embrace.

Words from My Belly Devotional

<u>Birth of Ministry</u>

Scripture: Acts 20:24: "But I count my life of no value to myself, so that I may finish my course and the ministry I received from the Lord Jesus, to testify to the gospel of GOD's grace."

Testimony

Everyone has a ministry within them. However, the birthing process is hard and long. We have to feed the ministry that is in our spiritual womb. Feed the ministry the Word of God, prayer, and relationship with the baby's Father, God Almighty. If we feed the ministry what it needs, you will have a "stillborn baby." The spiritual birth pangs are like no other. Once that baby is birthed, your purpose and destiny will become clearer.

WAIT

Wait on Me, wait on Me,
That is what the still small voice is telling me,
To renew your strength,
Lord, I have to repent,
Sometimes, patience is not my virtue,
I didn't mean to disappoint You,
Almighty God, You live in eternity,
I exist in time and that worries me,
Each second that goes by is a grain of sand of the hourglass of my life span,
Can I afford to roll the spiritual dice and stand?
If I let patience do its perfect work,
Between that time I might lose everything plus my shirt,
That still small voice is telling me, Oh ye of little faith,
How much convincing is it going to take?
I have delivered you from this, why you can't wait on that?
I designed your destiny, I have the map,
Stand still and see your salvation,
I didn't forsake you or take a vacation,
I never slumber or sleep,
Didn't I give you peace?
Wait on Me as I waited on you,
How can you forget I am God that brought you thought?
Lord, I will sit still,
If that is your prescription, then I will take the pill,
Waiting, waiting, waiting for my change to come,

I am going to lose it; I am not going to twiddle my thumbs,
I'll wait to renew my strength,
I will wait and be content,
I will wait.

Words from My Belly Devotional

Wait

Scripture: Isaiah 40:31: "[B]ut those who trust in the Lord will renew their strength; they will soar on wings like eagles; they will run and grow weary; they will walk and not faint."

Testimony

No one likes to wait, especially in the world we live in. We have to have it here and now. As much as I like to have my blessing and deliverance, I realize I am not on my time; I am on God's timing. When He has me waiting, He is teaching me patience. Sometimes, He doesn't answer my prayers right away because if He did, I will become a spoiled brat. Remember: good things come to those who wait on God.

Righteous Equation

If I add life plus myself and multiply it with trials and tribulations, then divide it by grace and mercy, then subtract my will and add God's will and increase faith to the 10th power, then life will be perpendicular to the square root of things hoped for. The result is that my latter will be greater than my past and less than my comprehension of carnal thoughts. Praise plus worship and carry the Spirit and truth equal His presence, parallel to the formula of relationship + fasting + praying + studying the Bible + good works + H2O (humility and obedience times two). This will result in a surplus of loving kindness and tender mercies, and then it will correlate into the sum of the whole of righteous.

Words from My Belly **Devotional**

Righteous Equation

Scripture: Romans 12:9–18: "Love must be without hypocrisy. Detest evil; cling to what is good. Show family affection to one another with brotherly love. Outdo one another in showing honor. Do not lack diligence in prayer. Share with the saints I their needs; pursue hospitality. Bless those who persecute you; bless and do not curse. Rejoice with those who rejoice; weep with those who weep. Be in agreement with one another. Do not be proud; instead, associate with the humble. Do not be wise in your own estimation. Do not repay anyone evil for evil. Try to do what is honorable in everyone's eyes."

Testimony

What I learned is that you need elements to live a righteous. You can't use one element to live holy. You can't just pray; you need a relationship with God plus read His Word. There are other elements needed. Once you get the elements, you can add on holiness, subtract baggage, and multiply spiritual blessings. You do the math.

My Rain

Drip, drop, drip, drop,
My eyes gaze upward,
It looks like the heavens are crying,
Is someone dying?
The rain is steady falling,
You can almost hear the earth calling,
Or crying out for relief,
Asking to be washed because of being tainted,
By this unrighteous picture being painted,
I am not stressing because the rain is a blessing,
The rain has come to restore,
Giving the earth more than enough,
But the rain is the representation of the anointing and the blood of Christ,
That guides and washes me whiter than snow,
Even those snow is cold,
It clears the air of infestation,
From corner to corner, from nation to nation,
When it is time for my graduation to heaven,
Then I know my task is complete like the biblical meaning for 7,
Be still and let the holy rain heal and deal with your situations,
Shower and drizzles don't mean pain,
It is joy and blessings, my rain.

Words from My Belly Devotional

My Rain

Scripture: Acts 14:17: "[A]lthough He did not leave Himself without a witness, since He did good; giving you rain from heaven and fruitful seasons, and satisfying your hearts with food and happiness."

Testimony

Most people do not like rainy days. Some may say it brings their mood down. If you think about it, if the rain did not fall, the grass, trees, and plants would not grow and be beautiful when it is sunny. Our water resources would have dried up, no drinking water, no bath, no showers, and the clothes and dishes will be still dirty. When the rainy days of life come, learn to receive them and know they prepare you for your sunny day in God.

MY REQUEST

My flesh is dying, dying while my spirit is crying, crying for the Father. I don't want Your hand not even a finger to be lifted from me, as a baby bird is close to its mother. Father, I long to stay under Your wing to sing a melody to please You. I may be a grown man, but when it comes to You, I am 100% child; in Your face I smile. Your joy is my strength, on my knees I repent, between the porch and the altar; my carnal clothes I rent, and Your word is heaven descended. Lord, help my help my spirit to rise. Jesus, you are the light that burns bright in me. Lord, shine through the carnality that is trying to suppress me daily. It always fails me; that is why I am crying out to Thee to be free to walk out my purpose and fulfill my destiny. Help me, Lord, please! Let not my heart and my mind to be deceived. I know I am saved by Your grace. Please, my Father, meet me at this place. Your mercy endures each morning I rise. Take me in Your arms right by Your loving, fatherly side.

Words from My Belly Devotional

My Request

Scripture: Philippians 4:6: "Don't worry about anything, through prayer and petition with thanksgiving; let your requests be made known to GOD."

Testimony

I know that I get tired of myself. I try to work on myself and fail every time. I didn't even pray for God to work on me. You have not because you ask not. So I asked the Lord to help me; I'd made my request to Him to work on me because He is the one who made me. God then told me what I must work on, and He helped me along the way because it was for His glory alone. God is still working on me; I realize this is a process. So I am encouraging you pray to God to work on you because it is very hard to do it alone.

RECOVERY OF MY TRINITY

This is a poem of recovery of my trinity,
Mind, body, and spirit,
Please allow me to break it down to you, so you can receive it,
I lose my mind when I allow the world's philosophies to enter my memories,
If my body is the temple of God and the dwelling place of the Holy Spirit,
Then I committed a sacrilege,
Defiling what is supposed to be holy,
Putting poisons of the streets in my blood and veins,
Ultimately messing up my brain,
I allow another to enter my temple, placing something not sacred on my altar,
My spirit is starving because I had not fed it, like a homeless pet,
I traded in my spirit for the sports car of worldly pleasures,
I can almost hear the knife ready to sever my connection between God and me,
Oh, how I miss my trinity,
Then a door of escape opened, so I took a chance,
Before I did that last dance with the devil,
I beheld God's celestial hand pointing me to a secret chamber,
Where there was a golden chest that rested on a table of white,
Curious to see what is inside,
On top, "Lost and Found" was inscribed,
I open the chest to find what was lost: my mind,
But now it's clear and defined,
Then my body was next,
Now it's healthy and not vexed,
And last, but not least, my spirit,

It's now strong and coherent in God's Word, verb for action,
With no fatal attraction to carnality,
With the three back in place,
I can run this race called saved,
Now I can testify on this day,
With the hand of God, He restored me,
With one conscious decision toward Him,
He has given me my recovery.

Words from My Belly Devotional

Recovery of My Trinity

Scripture: Joel 2:25: "And I will restore or replace for you the years that the locust has eaten-the hopping locust, the stripping locust, and the crawling locust, My great army which I sent among you."

Testimony

Have you ever felt out place with yourself? Your mind, body, and spirit were just off or out of balance, so much that you can't function. When I was in that state, I realize that it was my fault. I had let issues fester within me and let them stay in me too long. I was consumed with my issues and those of others; I was a mess. I was no good to myself or anybody else; I did more hurt than good. I went to God and pleaded with Him. I thanked Him for His mercy because He could just as easily leave me in the state that I was in. He cleared my mind, touched my hurting body, and breathed His breath of life into my spirit. To be honest, I was in this state three times in my life, just burned out, and I made a promise each time to not be that way again, but I always find myself back. The Lord had to teach me to slow down in all areas of my life so that the cares of life would not affect me so badly. I encourage you to balance your life; too much of anything, except for God's love, is a bad thing.

CLOTHE ME

As my spirit form walks in the garden of Your glory,
I hear a whisper in the wind which is Your breath,
Calling me to Your throne,
I stand before You naked,
In Your presence I am always naked, exposed,
My Father, when I leave Your presence clothes me in holiness,
Father, clothe me in a new priestly garment of praise,
Clothe me, oh Lord, for You are the only one who sees my exposure,
Clothe me with a sound mind with Your helmet,
Clothe me with Your breastplate of righteousness,
To protect my heart,
Shod my feet from the broken glass of shattered dreams,
Most importantly clothe me in Your glory,
For when the world sees me,
They will see Your love is my story,
Please, oh Lord, clothe me.

Words from My Belly Devotional

<u>Clothe Me</u>

Scripture: Revelation 3:5: "In the same way, the victor will be dressed in white clothes, and I will never erase his name from the book of life, but will acknowledge his name before My Father and before His angels."

Testimony

When I worship, I am naked before the Lord, but when I come out of worship, I ask the Lord to cover me. When you are in the Holy of Holies, you are safe in the presence of the Lord. Walking in this reality, you need to be covered with the armor of God and His fruit of the spirit. I don't have to tell you that life is hard and people are sometimes cruel. The armor and the spiritual blessings of the Lord can keep you. I ask, keep me, cover me, anoint me, shield me, teach me, and love me. In His presence I am exposed, but in this world, I want to be covered so that my faults and weakness will not be seen by the enemy or the people whom the enemy uses.

WHAT IS REAL?

What is real?
Is it something you can feel?
Is it an emotion?
Or is it an object that people can steal?
Lord, these mysteries please reveal,
So my mental equilibrium will be still,
This reality that is based on fact,
From my visual, it is just an act,
Everyday actors on the stage of life,
Try to hide who they are with all their might,
What is real?
These earthly concepts have things distorted,
To them, my spiritual vision I should have aborted,
If it is not tangible,
It is not reliable,
Looking Christian, the world's concepts sit back and laugh,
While deep in its own heart made a golden calf,
While not concerned with the aftermath,
What is real?
Does anyone know the score?
What is real, it's Righteousness, Encouragement, Anointing, and the Lord.

Words from My Belly Devotional

What Is Real?

Scripture: John 18:36: "'My kingdom is not of this world,' said Jesus. 'If My kingdom were of this world, My servants would fight, so that I wouldn't be handed over to Jews. As it is, My kingdom does not have its origin here.'"

Testimony

My thoughts often wonder about this world. The more I think of this world, the more I witness its falsehood. The world is two-faced, hypocritical, backstabbing selfish reality. So I ask myself what is real. Even those who call themselves Christians, they are holy on Sunday but worldly Monday through Saturday: one-day saints. It's bad enough the world is so-so—but the people of God! Sometimes, I pay attention to the world a little too much. I look to the Lord for what is real and can last long, things like His love, joy, peace, grace, mercy, kindness, and the blood of Jesus. To me that is what is real.

Where Is Your Fruit?

Are you growing?
Are you fruits showing?
If the Lord is looking for me when He is hungry,
I will not wither like the fig tree,
In the Word of God, Genesis 1:22, it implies,
To be fruitful and multiply,
To be fruit, there is no loophole in that command,
He wants us to grow and not settle,
Not to be traditional but take our walk to another level,
The soil has been spoiled because of lack of growth,
When a fresh Word from God comes,
The ground regurgitates, even chokes,
Break up the ground so a seed can be planted,
Harden not your heart like garnet,
Be broken before Him,
You can stand it,
Remove the rocks of pride,
Tear out the weeds of self,
Nurse that plant back to health.

Words from My Belly Devotional

<u>**Where Is Your Fruit?**</u>

Scripture: Matthew 7:17–18: "In the same way, every good tree produces good fruit, but a bad tree produces bad fruit. A good tree can't produce bad fruit; neither can a bad tress produce good fruit."

Testimony

Everyone is born with a seed; that seed could be gifts, talent, know-how, strength, speed, wisdom, or love. Like any seed, if you don't take care of it, it seed will not grow. There is something worse; you let it grow but neglect it, and it dies. Maybe you are trying to grow a seed on hardened surface, such as bitterness and depression. A seed can grow on good soil such as love, joy, and the rest of the fruits of the spirit. I know for myself I have to do some replanting because the ground of my heart wasn't right. I have to plant the seed that God had given me when my cold winter was over.

His Mirror

I was made to be a reflection of God. If that is true, then I am an organic mirror reflecting a celestial being. Then a voice of judgment spoke, "Mirror, mirror on the righteous wall, who will help you when you fall?" As soon as that sentence ended, stones of disobedience, trials, and tribulations came hurling toward my spiritual geographical location. Crash, break, just like that, my identity was shattered and scattered like exploding antimatter. Pieces of "self" turned into sand. Questions came knocking at the door of my mind. Will I ever be God's man again? Then the voice of truth spoke to me and said, "You can stand." With blood-soaked hands, He applied pressure to my sand. He rubbed the love of His blood in a 360-degree motion. Yes, He turned it around. He put me back together again. Suddenly, the Father looked upon me and saw His reflection. He hung me back on the wall of righteousness to bless and make a confession, that He is God and He made me His mirror, a reflection!

Words from My Belly Devotional

His Mirror

Scripture: Genesis 1:27: "So GOD created man in HIS own image; HE created him in the image of GOD; HE created male and female."

Testimony

Oftentimes I let the world affect who I am. For a great part of my life, I did not know who I am. I relied on people and the TV to dictate who I am; all the while I created a false image of myself. I thought that if I was like everybody else, I would fit in. The more I try to fit in, the more I don't; the spirit within me was rejecting what I was trying to put in. You all know that you can't fit something that doesn't belong. I did not fit in because I was designed in the image of God. God loves, not despises; He keeps His promises, not reneges; He forgives, not holds a grudge. Thanks to the blood of Jesus Christ, I am His reflection. Remember, you are a child of God and a child of the world.

Broken and Repenting

Lord, I have come, my sin made be spiritual numb!
So I press to be in place to chase You, my salvation,
I am in position between reality and eternity in a state of humility,
I cry out in the mist of Your glory!
Forgive me, Lord, restore me!
Forgive me, Father, for I have sinned!
Help me to turn away from it and never do it again!
I am begging You to do what you have to do!
I've depended on everything else but You!
I am here because I need to repent!
I need Your love and Your chastisement!
As my tear-soaked eyes look up,
I see the celestial hand of the Lord approach me,
With one touch, my trinity—mind, body, and spirit—shatters,
My broken being was scattered like ashes in the wind,
The fierce flames of trials and tribulation ignited on my fallen carcass,
The stench of carnality and slavery of my trinity fills the atmosphere,
Then God the Father breathed upon me,
Behold, a fresh fragrance emerges,
Then came a rumbling in my spirit,
The sinews of holiness integrated with my being,
In my mind, God is freeing my whole state of being,
In summary,
Once I was a glass filled with wine on the Father's table,
Then I fell and I was broken,
The prayer of repentance I had spoken,
He put me back together again with a heart that has been forgiven,
That is why it is okay to be broken and repenting.

Words from My Belly Devotional

Broken and Repenting

Scripture: Psalm 51:17: "The sacrifice pleasing to GOD is a broken spirit. GOD, You will not despise a broken and humbled heart."

Testimony

I have to live a lifestyle of repentance and brokenness. If I didn't live that lifestyle, I will get in the way of what God wants for my life. Sometimes my pride, selfishness, and anger will overtake my spirit to a point of spiritual numbness. What I mean by spiritual numbness is that you can't feel God or even operate in the spiritual realm. My praise and worship were dry. People know that you don't have a relationship with God. I knew that God can't use me if I am not humble, submitted, repenting, and serving. I have to press myself to get to God. The breaking was hard and it hurt, but I'd rather be in that state than not be in fellowship with God. I have to look at myself in the mirror, and I despise myself. Once you learn about yourself, the truth tastes bitter. During this process, I was exposed and talked about, but I had God to comfort me. All this was for my good because I have a purpose and destiny to fulfill, and I am accountable for it. I encourage you to repent and be broken before the Lord so He can use you mightily for His glory. Don't worry what people think of you; worry about what God thinks of you.

Thank You!

First, I'd like to give glory and honor to God and my Lord and Savior Jesus Christ. Without them, I would not be able to write poetry because He blessed me with that gift. I'd like to thank my mother, Violet Timpson, who loved me through the years and was always concerned about me even though I am a grown man. I love you, Mom! I'd like to thank my gorgeous, anointed, and encouraging wife, Rashieda Timpson. I love you, sweetie; you had my back when some turned theirs. I am truly blessed to have you as a wife. I would like to thank my spiritual father in the faith, Pastor Tyrone Smith, who believed in my gift. Thank you for your fathering, teaching, and support through the years; I am grateful. I'd like to thank Pastor Willie C. H. Garrett of the Solid Rock Church, Inc., for taking this lonely soul from Baltimore, Maryland, and letting me grow in your church. Thank you for your teaching, leadership, and love. God bless you, sir! Last but not least, I like to thank all of you who purchased this book, I pray that it will bless and encourage you that you are not alone in this walk. This book was designed to uplift you and to push you to your destiny. As we all know, we need a little push sometimes. Stay blessed, loved, and most of all, stay in God's presence and worship Him in Jesus's name!

Telly T. Timpson

CPSIA information can be obtained
at www.ICGtesting.com
Printed in the USA
BVHW081127070519
547593BV00003B/46/P